SEX, LOVE AND MARRIAGE

IN THE ELIZABETHAN AGE

SEX, LOVE AND MARRIAGE
IN THE ELIZABETHAN AGE

R. E. PRITCHARD

PEN & SWORD
HISTORY
AN IMPRINT OF PEN & SWORD BOOKS LTD.
YORKSHIRE – PHILADELPHIA

First published in Great Britain in 2021 by
PEN AND SWORD HISTORY
An imprint of
Pen & Sword Books Ltd
Yorkshire – Philadelphia

ISBN 978 1 52675 462 2

Typeset in Times New Roman 11.5/14 by
SJmagic DESIGN SERVICES, India.
Printed and bound by CPI Group (UK) Ltd, Croydon, CR0 4YY

Pen & Sword Books Limited incorporates the imprints of Atlas, Archaeology,
Aviation, Discovery, Family History, Fiction, History, Maritime, Military, Military
Classics, Politics, Select, Transport, True Crime, Air World, Frontline Publishing,
Leo Cooper, Remember When, Seaforth Publishing, The Praetorian Press,
Wharncliffe Local History, Wharncliffe Transport, Wharncliffe True Crime and
White Owl.

For a complete list of Pen & Sword titles please contact
PEN & SWORD BOOKS LIMITED
47 Church Street, Barnsley, South Yorkshire, S70 2AS, England
E-mail: enquiries@pen-and-sword.co.uk
Website: www.pen-and-sword.co.uk

Or

PEN AND SWORD BOOKS
1950 Lawrence Rd, Havertown, PA 19083, USA
E-mail: Uspen-and-sword@casematepublishers.com
Website: www.penandswordbooks.com

Contents

Introduction

It may seem rather odd, almost perverse, to write about sex, love and marriage in a time associated with, and ruled over by, a self-declared virgin queen with no personal, lived experience of any of these. Yet despite their ruler's largely self-imposed restrictions on her own life, and the efforts of the Church and the policing by the Church courts, Elizabeth's subjects seem to have engaged in surprisingly varied and even energetic sex lives.

Sir Francis Bacon, in his essay *Of Love*, observed that, 'The stage is more beholding to love than the life of man. For as to the stage, love is ever a matter of comedies, and now and then of tragedies; but in life it doth mischief, sometimes like a siren, sometimes like a fury.' All of these situations were described and evoked by Elizabethan writers in drama, prose and verse, commenting on and exploring the comedy and tragedy of Elizabethan sex and love lives.

Sir Francis concluded: 'Nuptial love maketh mankind; friendly love perfecteth it; but wanton love embaseth [debases] it.' Here, we shall see all of these. This brief survey will present them as lived by ordinary people, from the poorest working class to the gentry, and the hectic sex carousel of the Court and the troubled, frustrated life of the Queen herself. Whenever possible, the people of Elizabethan England will be quoted here directly, in their own words, in poems, plays, letters, sermons, journals – though mostly in modern spelling.

Chapter 1

Hearts on Fire

Love's Labours

It was a lover and his lass,
With a hey and a ho and a hey nonny no,
That through the green corn field did pass,
In the spring time, the only pretty ring time ...

Shakespeare could sing the Elizabethans' fantasies of romantic, pastoral love, as they liked to think of it; sometimes it was like that; often it was not. As it happens, within the charming emptiness here, 'hey nonny no' and 'ring' were also familiar euphemisms for the lass's genitals. For example, in the play, *The Wit of a Woman* (1604), a young woman's father complains about energetic, immodest dances: 'In such lavoltas [the women are lifted up to] mount so high, that you may see their hey, nonny, nonny no.' At the end of *The Merchant of Venice* (1596–7) there is excessively knowing play on the word 'ring', as Gratiano insists, 'While I live, I'll fear no other thing / So sore as keeping safe [newly-wed] Nerissa's ring.' The context makes the insinuation clear.

The period was remarkable for its outpouring of love writing. It was not that the writers and readers were all in love, rather, they were in love with the idea of being in love. The poems and songs, plays and romances, were all stories, expressions of feelings and exercises in wit and imagination, fictions with variable relationships with fact. For all that, they are invaluable in telling us what was going on in Elizabethans' minds, and also in giving us a fair idea of what was going on in reality.

Fulke Greville (1554–1628)[1] wrote a fine lyric on idealistic love, putting it in the context of the life force:

The nurse-life wheat within his green husk growing,
Flatters our hope, and tickles our desire,

Nature's true riches in sweet beauties showing,
Which set all hearts with labours love on fire …

Caelica, your youth, the morning of delight,
Enamelled o'er with beauties white and red,
All sense and thoughts did to belief invite,
That Love and Glory there are brought to bed;
    And your ripe years, Love's noon; he goes no higher,
    Turns all the spirits of Man into desire.

(There may have been no specific Caelica.)

This was probably written in the 1580s; by the 1590s Sir John Davies (1569–1626)[2] was impatient with all the poeticising of sex and courting:

Forsooth, wench, I cannot court thy sprightly eyes
With the base viol placed between my thighs;
I cannot lisp, nor to some fiddle sing,
Nor run upon a high-stretched minikin.

(The 'base viol' suggests the 'base vile' between his thighs; a minikin is a treble string, or a girl.)

I cannot whine in puling elegies,
Entombing Cupid in sad obsequies.
I am not fashioned for these amorous times,
To court thy beauty with lascivious rhymes.

(By 1592, Shakespeare's Richard III, 'not shaped for sportive tricks,/ Nor made to court an amorous looking-glass,' was impatient with 'the lascivious pleasing of a lute'.)

Davies concludes:

I cannot buss [kiss] thy foot, play with thy hair,
Swearing, 'By Jove, thou art most debonair.'
    Not I, by Cock [God], but shall I tell thee roundly,
    Hark in thine ear, zounds, I can (   ) thee soundly.

The omitted word – hardly ever printed – was monosyllabic. Neither writer was addressing an actual woman, but expressing an idea. Davies was mocking the clichés of courting.

Thomas Nashe (1567–1601) also parodied pretentious love poetry. In his novel *The Unfortunate Traveller* (1594), the hero of the story, page Jack, outwits his master in seduction:

> Who would have learned to write an excellent passion might have been a perfect tragic poet had he but attended half the extremity of his lament. Passion upon passion would throng one on another's neck. He would praise her beyond the moon and stars, and that so sweetly and ravishingly as I persuade myself he was more in love with his own curious-forming fancy than her face; and truth it is, many become passionate lovers only to win praise to their wits.
>
> He praised, he prayed, he desired and besought her to pity him that perished for her. From this his entranced mistaking could no man remove him. Who loveth resolutely will include everything under the name of his love. From prose he would leap into verse, and with these or suchlike rhymes assault her.

> If I must die, Oh, let me choose my death:
> Suck out my soul with kisses, cruel maid;
> In thy breasts' crystal balls embalm my breath;
> Dole it all out in sighs when I am laid.
> Thy lips on mine like cupping-glasses clasp,
> Let our tongues meet and strive as they would sting,
> Crush out my wind with one straight girting grasp,
> Stabs on my heart keep time whilst thou dost sing.
> Thy eyes like searing irons burn out mine,
> In thy fair tresses stifle me outright,
> Like Circe change me into loathsome swine,
> So I may live for ever in thy sight.
>> Into heaven's joys none can profoundly see,
>> Except that first they meditate on thee.

Sadly [seriously] and verily, if my master said true, I should, if I were a wench, make many men quickly immortal. What is't, what is't for a maid fair and fresh to spend a little lipsalve on a hungry lover? My master beat the bush and kept a coil and a prattling, but I caught the bird: simplicity and plainness shall carry it away in another world. God wot he was Petro Desperato when I, stepping to her with a Dunstable [plain] tale, made up my market. A holy requiem to their souls that think to woo a woman with riddles.

John Donne (1573–1631) also mocked fashionable love poetry, but shrewdly pointed out its advantages in *The Triple Fool*:

> I am two fools, I know,
> For loving, and for saying so
> In whining poetry.
> But where's that wise man that would not be I
> If she would not deny?

He was vigorous and brusque in his pursuit: 'For God's sake hold your tongue, and let me love.' In *Love's Progress*, he dismisses fancy love-sentiment, and declares bluntly:

> Whoever lives, if he do not propose
> The right true end of love, he's one that goes
> To sea for nothing but to make him sick.

It is not the woman's soul, or virtue, that he admires:

> Although we see celestial bodies move
> Above the earth, the earth we till and love:
> So we her airs contemplate, words and heart,
> And virtue, but we love the centric part.

In *To his Mistress, Going to Bed*, another poem from the 1590s, he is impatient and direct:

> Come, Madam, come, all rest my powers defy,
> Until I labour, I in labour lie.

> The foe oft-times, having the foe in sight,
> Is tired with standing, though he never fight …

She is urged to undress, and then to

> Licence my roving hands, and let them go
> Behind, before, above, between, below.
> O my America, my new found land,
> My kingdom, safeliest when with one man manned,
> My mine of precious stones, my empery,
> How blest am I in thus discovering thee …

After all,

> Full nakedness, all joys are due to thee.
> As souls unbodied, bodies unclothed must be
> To taste whole joys …

He concludes:

> To teach thee, I am naked first; why then,
> What need'st thou have more covering than a man?

While several writers satirised fashionable love poetry and love-making, a few condemned them as morally degenerate. None more so than John Marston (1576–1634), a satiric poet and dramatist, who managed to combine in his writing energy, obscurity, obscenity and morality (not something everyone could do). After a lively career as a poet (his satires, like those of his contemporaries, were burned by order of the bishops in 1599), dramatist and theatre manager, scoffed at in turn by Ben Jonson for his red hair and little legs, he was eventually ordained as a priest. His volume *The Scourge of Villainy* (1596) tore into the affectations of his fellow writers. One, condemning the current obsession with sex, begins,

> What should I say? Lust hath confounded all,
> The bright gloss of our intellectual
> Is foully soiled. The wanton wallowing
> In fond delights, and amorous dallying

> Hath dusked the fairest splendour of our soul:
> Nothing now left, but carcase, loathsome foul.

In another poem he derides the fantasies of other poets, outbidding each other with absurdities:

> O frantic fond pathetic passion!
> Is't possible such sensual action
> Should clip the wings of contemplation? ...
> Saturio wished himself his mistress' busk,   [corset]
> That he might sweetly lie, and softly lusk   [lie hidden]
> Between her paps. But out on Phrygio
> That wished he were his mistress' dog, to go
> And lick her milk-white fist, o pretty grace.
> Parthenophil, thy wish I will omit,
> So beastly 'tis, I may not utter it.

[The following extract refers to a sonnet by Barnabe Barnes, where the speaker wishes to be his mistress's glove or necklace: 'Or that sweet wine, which down her throat doth trickle, / To kiss her lips, and lie next her heart, / Run through her veins, and pass by Pleasure's part ...]

> Here's one would be a flea, jest comical,
>   Another his sweet lady's farthingale,
>   To kiss her tender breech ...

Not all love poetry was grovelling or would-be witty. There was also happy and mutual love, as in Philip Sidney's (1554–1586) charming lyric, spoken by the woman in *Song* from *Arcadia*:

> My true love hath my heart, and I have his,
> By just exchange one for the other given.
> I hold his dear, and mine he cannot miss:
> There never was a better bargain driven.

Conversely, there was also poetry of failed mutual love, as in the touching poem, by Michael Drayton (1563–1631)[3], of the unwilling break-up of a romance:

6

Since there's no help, come let us kiss and part,
Nay, I have done, you get no more of me,
And I am glad, yea glad with all my heart,
That thus so cleanly I my self can free;
Shake hands for ever, cancel all our vows,
And when we meet at any time again,
Be it not seen in either of our brows,
That we one jot of former love retain.
Now, at the last gasp of Love's failing breath,
When, his pulse failing, Passion speechless lies,
When Faith is kneeling by the bed of death,
And Innocence is closing up his eyes,
 Now if thou would'st, when all have given him over,
 From death to life, thou might'st him yet recover.

*   *   *   *   *

Fair Game

Not everyone had love, or even marriage, in mind (except some young women) and were merely playing the field, for what they might catch. In the verse dialogue, *The Bride*, by Samuel Rowlands (1570–1630), one young woman sadly observes that there are too many

Chaste bachelors that never mean to match,
Who for the single life smooth tales have told,
And yet the fleshly knaves will have a snatch:
I'll ne'er trust those that of themselves do boast,
The great precisians [puritans] will deceive you most …

One such swaggering boaster is denounced in Middleton and Dekker's play, *The Roaring Girl* (1611), by Moll Cutpurse:

       Th'art one of those
That thinks each woman thy fond flexible whore,
If she but cast a liberal eye upon thee,
Turn back her head, she's thine, or amongst company
By chance drink first to thee: then, she's quite gone,

7

There's no means to help her: nay, for a need,
Wilt swear unto thy credulous fellow lechers
That th'art more in favour with a lady
At first sight than her monkey all her lifetime.
How many of our sex, by such as thou
Have their good thoughts paid with a blasted name,
That never deserved loosely or did trip
In path of whoredom, beyond cup or lip.
But for [except for] the stain of conscience and of soul,
Better had women fall into the hands
Of an act silent, than a bragging nothing.
There's no way out.

It appears that sexual harassment was extremely common; historian Bernard Capp suggests that

> men at every social level … regarded any unaccompanied female as fair game, and contemporary ideas about women's sexual drive and moral frailty encouraged them to assume that any target would quickly succumb to persuasion or pressure … . When George Ball accosted a woman at Chesterton, Cambridgeshire, in 1599, aware that her husband had been away for several months, he allegedly took out his penis and informed her, 'Thou art quite lost for want of such a thing as this.'

Some men seemed genuinely bewildered if they found themselves rebuffed,[4] and this behaviour could easily slide into assault and rape. In 1570, Bridget Pakeman said that her employer, Thomas Sayer, a parson

> would have ravished her, first flattering and embracing her when she was turning a flooring of malt [households frequently did their own brewing], and promised her if his wife died of child he would marry her, and attempted to handle her shamefully, taking up her clothes. Another time on the kiln as she was heaving of malt, at which time using her as before … . And another time about midsummer, she having gathered up a bundle of rushes … Sayer came to her,

8

and did shamefully use her, at which time she was forced to take him by the members to save herself, whereon Sayer gave her a blow on the ear and therewith departed.

The churchwarden presented the case before the Church court, and the case was dragged out until she gave up and went away. Fourteen years later, Sayer was accused of rape.[5]

A straightforward case of rape – or so it seemed – came before the assize court in 1590, when Joan Somers said that:

upon a certain working day, happening about Christmas last, she being in a ploughed field serving of her dame's cattle, Rice Evans came unto her, and told her that she might now cry her heart out before anybody could hear her cry, and so indeed as she saith, he did violently abuse her body and committed fornication unto her.

However, the Church court accused her of fornication.[6]

In 1618, M. Dalton's *The Countrey Justice* provided magistrates with useful guidance on judging rape cases:

To ravish a woman where she doth neither consent before nor after is a felony [a capital offence]. But a woman that is ravished ought presently [promptly] to levy hue and cry, or to complain presently to some credible persons … . If the woman at the time of the supposed rape do conceive with child by the ravisher, this is no rape, for a woman cannot conceive with child except she do consent [a variation on contemporary medical thinking, which believed orgasm was necessary for conception[7]]. If a man ravish a woman who consenteth for fear of death or duress, yet this is a ravishment against her will, for that consent ought to be voluntary and free … . It is a good plea, in an appeal of rape, to say that before the ravishment supposed, she was his concubine… and yet to ravish a harlot against her will is felony … . The taking away of a maid under sixteen years of age without the consent of her parents … or deflowering her, is no felony, but yet shall be punished with long imprisonment without bail, or grievous fine. But unlawfully and carnally to know and abuse any woman child under the age of ten years is felony, although such child consent before.

* * * * *

Gentle Ganymede

Sexual activity, however irregular and ostensibly condemned, might be carried on quite ostentatiously, and be surprisingly varied. In his fourth satire, Donne touches on Court extravagance, and meets a gossipy courtier, 'Who wastes in meat, in clothes, in horse, he notes; / Who loves whores, who boys, and who goats.' Predictably, Marston also picks up on reported fashionable tastes in whores, boys and bestiality (the last, surely, must have been very uncommon). In his *Satire 3*, he tells of a serious, worried father who has forced his wastrel son to

> clean forsake his Pickthatch drab.   [brothel whore]
> Alack, alack, what piece of lustful flesh
> Hath Luscus left, his priape [lust] to redress?
> Grieve not, good soul, he hath his Ganymed,   [rent boy]
> His perfumed she-goat, smooth-combed and high fed.
> At Hogsdon [Hoxton – hog's den, a notorious pick-up place]
>   now his monstrous lust he feasts,
> For there he keeps a bawdy-house of beasts … .
> Faith, what cares he for fair Cynedian boys,
> Velvet-capped goats, Dutch mares? Fut, but common toys.
> Detain them all, on this condition,
> He best may use the Cynic friction [masturbation].
> O now ye male stews, I can give pretence
> For your luxurious incontinence …

Male homosexuality was well known about at the time, but people kept quiet about it, especially as anal intercourse was a felony (although it was used contraceptively). One unlucky yeoman from Hoxton was executed for buggery. The educated classes were very familiar with homosexual sentiment, as it was a frequent topic in the classical texts – especially the Greek – which constituted a large part of their schooling. Pastoral lyrics

10

deriving from the classical tradition, insofar as they dealt with love between shepherds and shepherd boys, enabled the poetic description of homosexual, or homophile, romance. Christopher Marlowe's famous romantic lyric, 'Come live with me and be my love' from *The Passionate Shepherd to His Love* (1599), is spoken by a shepherd to his male beloved – no shepherdess. In Edmund Spenser's *The Shepheardes Calender* (1579), the shepherd Hobbinol is in love with the shepherd Colin Clout, who complains that 'my love he seek[s] with dayly suit', and Hobbinol reports how 'whilome on him was all my care and joye,/ Forcing with gyfts to winne his wanton heart.'

Going upmarket, socially, in Marlowe's *Dido, Queen of Carthage* (early; printed 1594), Jupiter woos the youth Ganymede – 'Come, gentle Ganymede and play with me / I do love thee well' – even giving him his wife's jewels to 'trick thy arms and shoulders with my theft', for which the lad promises to 'hug with you an hundred times'. Dealing with Court life, in Marlowe's *Edward II* (1592), a courtier, Gaveston, plans how he will seduce the king:

> Music and poetry is his delight;
> Therefore I'll have Italian masques by night;
> Sweet speeches, comedies and pleasing shows;
> And in the day, when he shall walk abroad,
> Like sylvan nymphs my pages shall be clad;
> My men, like satyrs grazing on the lawns,
> Shall with their goat feet dance an antic hay;
> Sometimes a lovely boy in Dian's shape,
> With hair that gilds the water as it glides,
> Crownets of pearls about his naked arms,
> And in his sportful hands an olive tree,
> To hide those parts which men delight to see …

Playwrights often exploited the ambiguous effects of boys/youths playing women characters. What might be thought of as homophile relationships may be found in several of Shakespeare's comedies. In *As You Like It*, Rosalind, played by a boy, dressing as a youth taking the name Ganymede and acting as a woman, Orlando finds himself responding to this young man – as, in a sense, he is. Frequently, boys played women playing boys wooing women, played by boys. In *Twelfth Night*, Viola woos Olivia, with unsettling effect, as, still in male dress, she unnerves Count Orsino. Also notable is the strong affection of the sea captain Antonio for young Sebastian (as pretty as his twin, Viola), which leads him to risk the death penalty. Another Antonio in *The Merchant of Venice*, seems unduly sad in his unexpressed love for Bassanio, telling him, 'My purse, my person, my extremest means / Lie all unlocked to your occasions.' Why do Jessica and Nerissa escape from Shylock dressed as boys? Fortunately, Lorenzo welcomes his beloved dressed in 'the lovely garnish of a boy'. Portia and Nerissa dress as youths and when Portia says, 'I'll prove the prettier fellow of the two … . And speak the change of man and boy / With a reed voice, and turn two mincing steps / Into a manly stride,' she emphasises what the boy actor has to do.

In Ben Jonson's *Epicoene* (1609), a sour comedy very much concerned with sexual ambivalence, a pageboy dressed as a woman complains how, 'The gentlewomen play with me, and throw me o'the bed; and carry me into my lady, and she kisses me with her oiled face [with cosmetics]; and puts a peruke on my head; and asks me if I will wear her gown, and I say no.' The appeal of this episode seems particularly perverse, in a perverse play.

More straightforward expressions of homosexual love could be found in several poems, even if they weren't widely distributed. A notable example is in the sonnet sequence *Cynthia* (1595) by Richard Barnfield (1574–1627). Sonnet II has a surprise for one young man:[8]

> Sighing, and sadly sitting by my love,
> He asked the cause of my heart's sorrowing,
> Conjuring me by heaven's eternal king,
> To tell the cause which me so much did move.
> Compelled, quoth I, to thee I will confess,
> Love is the cause, and only love it is
> That doth deprive me of my heavenly bliss.
> Love is the pain that doth my heart oppress.
> And what is she, quoth he, whom thou dost love?
> Look in this glass, quoth I, there thou shalt see
> The perfect form of my felicity.
> When, thinking that it would strange magic prove,
> He opened it [a locket]: and taking off the cover,
> He straight perceived himself to be my lover.

Barnfield is sometimes more sexually suggestive. His *The Affectionate Shepherd* (1594), itself dedicated to Penelope, Lady Rich (for what that's worth), exploits the pastoral convention in the story of shepherd Daphnis wooing and seducing Ganimede. At sight of 'that fair boy that had my heart entangled, Cursing the time, the place, the sense, the sin;/ I came, I saw, I viewed, I slipped in.' His 'viewed' suggests Caesar's 'conquered'; he suggests that he slipped into sin, but physical penetration is implicit. In another sonnet he develops the idea of Ganimede as a bee, to imply an invitation to fellatio and more:

> Then shouldst thou suck my sweet and my fair flower,
> That now is ripe, and full of honey-berries:
> Then would I lead thee to my pleasant bower
> Filled full of grapes of mulberries and cherries …

Elsewhere, he pleads for the lad's sexual surrender, when, with obvious genital metaphors, he writes how, as a love pilgrim, 'I'd hang a bag and bottle at thy back.'

Barnfield himself later insisted that, although 'some there were that did interpret *The Affectionate Shepherd* otherwise than in truth I meant … . Only this I will unshadow my conceit: being nothing else but an imitation of Vergil in the second Eclogue, of Alexis.' Alan Bray, quoting Barnfield, writes that such verses should not be assumed to be 'the product of personal experience. Like other self-consciously classical poetry of this kind, they were the product of a literary genre which (if it was more than a mere exercise) was about friendship, the "insensible part" of love, not sexuality but a Platonic meeting of minds.' There does not seem to be much of any platonic meeting of minds; and, for merely a protracted literary exercise, the sense of sexual desire is strongly expressed.

It is clear that Shakespeare had read Barnfield, and echoes and adapts his phrasing in his own sonnets addressed to a young man; but where Barnfield is more suggestive of a physical consummation, Shakespeare is concerned with exploring emotional possession – and love.

When Barnfield's Daphnis contrasts his feelings of love with his sexually rapacious rival, Gwendolin, he declares, 'I love thee for thy gifts, she for her pleasure,/ I for thy virtue, she for beauty's treasure'. In Shakespeare's *Sonnet 20*, which is addressed to a young man – 'the master-mistress of my passion' – he complains that nature has frustrated him, by 'adding one thing to my purpose nothing', so that 'Mine be thy love, and thy love's use their treasure.'

The homosexual element in Shakespeare's sonnet sequence would have been noticed, but was not openly commented on in print. Though the sequence was mostly written in the 1590s, it was not printed until 1609.

* * * * *

A Naughty House

In *Measure for Measure*, Constable Elbow describes Mistress Overdone's establishment as 'a naughty house', meaning a stew or brothel. Marston, in his *Satire 3*, refers to stews (so called because they were bathhouses before they became brothels) and says men who could not manage seduction or bring themselves to rape went to the professionals. Brothels and prostitutes were frequent in the less officially controlled parts of London. Foreign visitors, such as Thomas Platter in 1559, remarked on them:

> Since the city is very large, open and populous, watch is kept every night in all the streets, so that misdemeanours shall be punished. Good order is kept in the city in the matter of prostitutes, for which special committees are set up, [when] they punish the men with imprisonment and fines. The woman is taken to Bridewell, the King's palace, situated near the river, where the executioner scourges her naked before the populace.

That might have appealed to some spectators. In his frenzy, King Lear cries out:

> Thou rascal beadle, hold thy bloody hand.
> Why dost thou lash that whore? Strip thy own back;
> Thou hotly lusts to use her in that kind
> For which thou whip'st her.

The watch might not always be as rigorous as Platter suggests, and be more like the dozy or corrupt watchmen figured in several comedies, including *Measure for Measure*.

14

Many prostitutes were to be found outside the city walls, in Petticoat Lane, Smithfield, Clerkenwell and Limehouse (convenient for the dock area). Others were over the river in the Bankside of Southwark, in the area formerly owned by the Bishop of Winchester, which led to the phrase 'Winchester goose', slang for a diseased Southwark whore – or her client. The area also held the bear-baiting hall, Paris Garden, and several theatres, in which several notable figures of the theatre community were involved. Philip Henslowe, theatre manager, and his son-in-law, the celebrated actor Edward Alleyn, both associates of Shakespeare, ran brothels in Bankside: the Barge, the Bell, the Cock and the Unicorn. In 1593, Alleyn, when out of town, wrote to his first wife, Joan about the common punishment for brothel bawds: 'Mouse, I little thought to hear that which I now hear by [about] you, for it is well known that they say that you were, by my Lord Mayor's office, made to ride in a cart, you and all your fellows.' When Joan died, her property was transferred to the marriage settlement of his second wife, Constance, daughter of Dr John Donne, Dean of St Paul's. Small world.

There were many ways of profiting from the sex industry. Samuel Rowlands has a comic warning story of 'cony-catching' – cheating the naïve – in his 1602 tale, *A Whore that Cross-bit [swindled] a Gentleman of the Inns of Court.*[9] While fictional, there are enough similar stories to suggest that the practice was not uncommon:

> A certain quean belonging to a close nunnery about Clerkenwell, lighting in the company of a young puny [novice] of the Inns of Court, trained him home with her ... there covenanting for so much to give him his houseroom all night. To bed they went together like man and wife. At midnight a crew of her copesmates kept a knocking and bustling at the door. She, starting suddenly out of her sleep, arose and went to the window to look out; wherewith she, crying out to him, said that a Justice was at the door with a company of bills [halberdiers] and came to search for a [Catholic] seminary priest, and that there was no remedy but she must open unto them. Wherefore either he must rise and lock himself to a study that was hard by, or they should be both carried to Bridewell. The poor silly youth in a trance, suffered her to lead him whither she would, who

hastily thrust him into the study, and there locked him, and went to let them in.

Then entered Sim Swashbuckler, Captain Gogswounds and Lawrence Longswordsman, with their appurtenances, [and] made enquiry, as if they had been officers indeed, for a young seminary priest that should be lodged there that night. She simpered it, and made curtsy, and spake reverently to them, as if she had never seen them before and that they had been such as they seemed, and told them she knew of none such and that none lay there but herself. With that, through signs that she made, they spied where his clothes were fallen down between the chest and the wall. Then they began to rail upon her, and call her a thousand whores, saying they would make her an example, aye, marry would they, and use her like an infidel for her lying, nor would they stand searching any longer, but she would be constrained to bring him forth; and that they might be sure he should not start, they would carry away his clothes with them. As for the closet, because it was a gentleman's out of town, they would not rashly break it open, but they would set watch and ward about the house till the morning, by which time they would resolve further what to do. So out of doors go they with his clothes, doublet, hose, hat, rapier, dagger, shoes, stockings and twenty marks which he was to pay upon a bond the next day for his father, to a merchant in Canning Street, and left Nicholas Novice starving and quaking in that doghole.

The morning grew on, and yet the young ninnyhammer, though he was almost frozen to death, stood still and dare not stir, till at length the goodwife of the house came and let him out, and bade him shift for himself, for the house was so belayed [besieged] that it was not possible for him to escape, and that she was utterly undone through his coming thither. After many words it grew to this upshot, that he must give her a ring worth thirty shillings, which he then had on his finger, only to help him out at a back door, and in so doing she would lend him a blanket to cast about him. Which being performed, like an Irish beggar he departed on the backside of the fields to his chamber, vowing never to pay so dear for one night's lodging during his life.

Apart from such exercises in private enterprise, the main sex business was in open brothels. Thomas Dekker wrote about 'our unclean sisters' in Shoreditch, Southwark, Westminster and Clerkenwell, describing how 'the doors of notorious carted bawds like Hell Gates stand night and day open, with a pair of harlots in taffeta gowns, like two painted posts, garnishing out these doors, being better to the house than a double sign.' Thomas Nashe waxed even more fiercely eloquent (and, no doubt, profitably) on the subject in his *Christ's Tears over Jerusalem* (1593):

> London, what are thy suburbs but licensed stews? Can it be so many brothel-houses of salary sensuality and sixpenny whoredom (the next door to the magistrates) should be set up and maintained, if bribes did not bestir them? I accuse none, but certainly justice somewhere is corrupted. Whole hospitals of ten-times-a-day dishonested strumpets have we cloistered together. Night and day entrance to them is as free as to a tavern.
>
> Not one of them but hath a hundred retainers … . No Smithfield ruffianly swashbuckler will come off with such harsh hell-raking oaths as they. Every one of them is a gentlewoman and either the wife of two husbands or a bed-wedded bride before she was ten years old. The speech-shunning sores and sight-irking botches of their insatiate intemperance they will unblushingly lay forth and jestingly brag of, wherever they haunt. To church they never repair … . Awake your wits, grave and authorized law-distributors, and show yourselves as insinuative-subtle in smoking this city-sodoming trade out of his starting-hole as the professors of it are in underpropping it.

As it was, the city authorities resented his criticisms and insinuations, and put him in Newgate Prison for a while, unfortunately during a plague epidemic. Intermittent efforts were indeed made to deal with brothels and prostitution. In 1603, the authorities determined to clear the slums, partly because of fear of infection from the plague and partly because of the brothels, and sent the women and their pimps to Bridewell Prison. In *Measure for Measure*, the bawd Mistress Overdone and her pimp, Pompey Bum, complain that 'all the houses in the suburbs of Vienna [London] must be plucked down.' Yet some corruption remains. When she asks about the brothels in the City, Pompey says, 'They shall stand for seed; they had gone down too, but that a wise burgher put in for them.' They remain confident that their business will continue, if only in 'a hot-house, which, I think, is a very ill house too,' adds Constable Elbow. Brothels were not, of course, confined to London; in 1571, in West Ham, then outside the capital, a woman was accused of being a bawd, 'a maintainer of two men's wives', where she 'had a glass like unto a pintle and a pair of ballocks for guests to drink in.'

Moralistic denunciation always pays well; on the other hand, titillating stories could also be profitable. Ironically, at about the same time as writing *Christ's Tears*, Thomas Nashe also wrote entertainingly about a visit to a brothel in *The Choice of Valentines* (before 1594),[10] an interesting poem (though not included in most anthologies) that, in its way, has a lot to say about male Elizabethan sexual attitudes and anxieties. Literally, it could be described as pornographic – the word derives from Greek, meaning, writing about whores – though really it belongs with other, more literary erotic poems, such as Shakespeare's *Venus and Adonis* (1593) or Marlowe's *Hero and Leander* (1598), which were designed to entertain rather than to excite.

In his prefatory poem to his patron, Ferdinando Stanley, Lord Strange, Nashe writes how

> Complaint and praises every one can write,
> And passion-out their pangs in stately rhymes,
> But of love's pleasures none did ever write
> That hath succeeded in these latter times.

He begins in a pseudo-Chaucerian vein, evoking rural courtship practices, which could still be seen (there is perhaps no better picture of Elizabethan courting):

> It was the merry month of February,
> When young men in their jolly roguery

Rise early in the morn 'fore break of day
To seek them valentines so trim and gay,
With whom they may consort in summer sheen,
And dance the heydegays on our town green
At ales at Easter or at Pentecost,
Perambulate the fields that flourish most,
And go to some village a-bordering near
To taste the cream, and cakes and such good cheer,
Or see a play of strange morality
Shown by bachelors of Manningtree,   [in Essex]
Whereto the country franklins flock-meal swarm,
And John and Joan come marching arm in arm,
Even on the hallows of that blessed saint ...

He combines nostalgia with condescension: a townie writing for a townie. His narrator, Tomalin, tries for a note of Petrarchist love-idealism – 'I went, poor pilgrim, to my lady's shrine' – only to find that she has moved away: implicitly, she has been whoring, and, chivvied by the justices, has 'shifted to an upper ground' (a notable brothel area in Southwark). Here he has to deal with 'a foggy three-chinned dame', the bawd, who, after he has paid a deposit, leads him to 'a shady loft / Where Venus' bouncing vestals skirmish oft.' However, he wants only his beloved Francis, for whom he must pay more, who 'in her velvet gowns /And ruffs, and periwigs as fresh as May / Cannot be kept with half a crown a day.'

She arrives, and they embrace, and he describes her body, with its

Pretty rising womb [*sic*] without a weam [blemish],
That shone as bright as any silver stream;
And bare out like the bending of an hill,
At whose decline a fountain dwelleth still,
That hath his mouth beset with ugly briars,
Resembling much a dusky net of wires.

Such landscape metaphors, of the fecund garden mount and stream, were used by other poets (in 'stately rhymes') such as Spenser in *The Faerie Queene* (1590), describing the moist Mount of Venus (or mons veneris) in the Garden of Adonis (III.vi); the net of hairs is used

19

elsewhere to suggest traps, as by the witch in The Bower of Bliss (II.xii). Unfortunately, Tomalin is over-excited and now cannot perform: 'So are my limbs unwieldy for the fight, / That spend their strength in thought of her delight.' The verb 'spend' for ejaculation was common at the time – 'th'expense of spirit' – with its suggestion of loss and male weakening, at the expense of satisfying the woman's stronger sexuality. (One might think of Botticelli's *Venus and Adonis*, where she reclines complacently while he, disarmed, lies back, exhausted.)

Her vigorous assistance helps him to perform, satisfactorily for them both: 'No tongue may tell the solace that she feels.' Interestingly, she is imaged as a (female) sun, the god Phoebus, so reversing their traditional male roles. After her climax, she wants more, but finding that his 'well is dry', turns to her trusty dildo. (Nashe's use of the word antedates the OED's earliest citation.) Such instruments are described at some length: 'Attired in white velvet or in silk, / And nourished with hot water or with milk; / And otherwise in thick congealed glass.' This is a great success for her, though Tomalin, 'not as Hercules the stout, / That to the seventh journey could hold out,' and now apparently made redundant, curses it, before leaving 'lean and lank as any ghost'. Though at the end Nashe apologises to his patron for his 'lascivious wit', the poem is not, as a reader might have expected, a genial celebration of male conquest and satisfaction, but more of a worry about female exploitation and sexual superiority.

There may even have been male brothels for women (who usually could manage well enough without). Bathhouses could serve double purposes. In Francis Osborne's play of around 1654, entitled *The True Tragi-comedie Formerly Acted at Court* and based on the scandalous murder of Thomas Overbury, there is a reference to such places as Madame Caesar's, 'or the Captain's wife in Aldersgate Street, that was the first that kept a male stews, whither the greatest she's in England came under pretence of eating Apricocks ungelt.' The pun on a prick is obvious; the cock would be ungelt, not gelded or castrated, but with its stones. In *Measure For Measure*, Pompey Bum has a rambling story about a woman coming to the house for two stewed prunes with their stones in a dish. Giles Fletcher's comedy, *The Custom of the Country* (c. 1619), has scenes of the male whores in a women's brothel (the owner claims, 'my custom is with young ladies / And high-fed City dames') complaining of exhaustion from overwork: 'the labour was so much', and 'I'll no more whoring: This fencing 'twixt a pair of sheets, more wears one than all the exercise in the world besides.'[11]

Some young women got drawn into part-time prostitution by bullying, unscrupulous employers. Emma Finch told the governors of Bridewell how her mistress, Alice Robinson, a tavern owner, 'would oftentimes force her to go up into a room to be naught with divers men', as, for example, the instance of

> a bricklayer who came to the house for a pot of beer, and later sent for an eel pie, which they [the Robinsons] ate and then he would have a pint of wine, which the master himself went for, and in that time when her master was gone for the wine, her mistress caused her to go up to the bricklayer, and there the said bricklayer had the use and carnal knowledge of her body, and he gave her eighteen pence which her mistress took from her as soon as the bricklayer was gone away.[12]

Some settled for this kind of work, despite the risk of disease and punishment, as it was more profitable than an ordinary job. A prostitute would normally earn between four and fifteen shillings a time, depending on how much the bawd kept. It has been suggested that apprentices might pay an average of one shilling and ten pence, and other men five shillings and eight pence.

Financial difficulties drove some married women or widows into occasional prostitution. John Marston's witty, independently minded character, Freevill, in *The Dutch Courtesan* (1604) defends them:

> Alas, good creatures, what would you have them do? Would you have them get their living by the curse of man, the sweat of their brows? So they do; every man must follow his trade, and every woman her [sexual] occupation. A poor decayed mechanical man's [manual worker's] wife, her husband is laid up; may not she lawfully be laid down, when her husband's only rising is by his wife's falling? A captain's wife wants means; her commander lies in

open field abroad; may not she be in civil arms at home? A waiting gentlewoman that had wont to take say [fine cloth] to her lady, miscarries or so: the Court misfortune throws her down; may not the City courtesy take her up? Do you know no alderman would pity such a woman's case? Why is charity grown a sin? Or relieving the poor and impotent an offence? You will say beasts take no money for their fleshly entertainment; true, because they are beasts, therefore beastly. Only men give to lose, because they are men, therefore manly; and indeed, wherein should they bestow their money better? In land, the title may be cracked; in houses, they may be burned; in apparel, 'twill wear; in wine, alas for pity, our throat is but short. But employ your money upon women, and a thousand to one some one of them will bestow that on you shall stick by you as long as you live. They are no ungrateful persons; they will give you quit for quo; do ye protest, they'll swear; do you rise, they'll fall; do you fall, they'll rise; do you give them the French crown, they'll give you the French [French coin; bald patch caused by the pox] – *O justus, justa, justum*. They sell their bodies; do not better persons sell their souls? Nay, since all things have been sold, honour, justice, faith, nay, even God himself,

> Ay me, what base ignobleness is it
> To sell the pleasure of a wanton bed?

Certainly, some people did very well out of the sex business, as Samuel Rowlands shows, in his verse *Doctor Merrie-man* (1609). After initial good cheer, a successful brothel owner reveals a darker world:

> I am a professed courtesan,
> That live by people's sin:
> With half a dozen punks I keep,
> I have great comings in.
> Such store of traders haunt my house,
> To find a lusty wench,
> That twenty gallants in a week

Do entertain the French;
Your courtier and your citizen,
Your very rustic clown,
Will spend an angel on the pox,
Even ready money down … .
Some go to Houndsditch with their cloth[e]s
To pawn for money-lending,
And some I send to surgeons' shops,
Because they lack some mending … .
The world is hard, all things are dear,
Good-fellowship decays,
And every one seeks profit now
In these same hungry days … .
For seeing I do venture fair,
At price of whipping cheer,
I have no reason but to make
My customers pay dear

Some did very well; but others, as Rowlands points out, paid a heavy
price.

* * * * *

After Venus, Mercury

The note of fear and warning of the syphilis, otherwise known as the pox
or the French disease, is like a constant, background drumbeat in serious
or comic accounts of irregular sexual activity in Elizabethan London.

There was no shortage of warnings. A ballad, *The whoremongers
conversion and his exhortation*, urges men:

Then scorn those painted counterfeits
That get their means by wicked sleights,
They'll learn you so much parley French,
From you shall come a rotten stench,
And at last you shall be forced to fall
i'the surgeon's hands, o'th Hospital:
There you shall lie and rot,

> This is by whoring got,
> Then good your worship use it not.

Syphilis, caused by the spirochaete *Treponema pallidum*, appears to have arrived in England in the fifteenth century, but didn't figure prominently until the middle and later sixteenth century.

It was called *morbus neapolitanus* by the French, who believed it originated in Italy, and *morbus gallicus* by the Italians, who considered it to be French. The English also called it 'the French disease'. In 1579, William Clowes (c. 1540-1604), a surgeon at St Bartholomew's and Christ's hospitals published his guide, *A Short and Profitable Treatise Touching the Disease Called (Morbus Gallicus)*. Apart from urging his readers to avoid fornication and calling for severe punishments for those engaged in the sex trade, his treatment consisted largely of a controlled diet, which did little to deal with the problem. From its early years, the main treatment as applied by barber surgeons generally, was the use of mercury, either by swallowing, spreading as an ointment, or breathing in the fumes with one's head covered in a hood in the 'hot-house'; an extremely unpleasant experience that might last several days. Notoriously, early in the seventeenth century, William Davenant, a Court poet, acquired 'a terrible clap of a black [dark] handsome wench that lay in Axe-Yard, Westminster' (as John Aubrey recorded in his *Brief Lives*). That, and clumsy treatment by mercury, rotted away part of his nose.

The treatment remained standard for many years, but was of limited effect. It was reasonably helpful in the early stages, clearing up the most obvious sores and lesions, but was less effective in the secondary stages and, unfortunately, continued use proved poisonous. Various symptoms ensued. Mercury ate into the flesh, even more than the syphilis; the throat might be infected and teeth might drop out. One symptom was loss of hair, as Thomas Lodge observed in his satire, *A Fig for Momus* (1595), on encountering an unhappy friend:

> He wore a silken night-cap on his head,
> And looked as if he had been lately dead.
> I asked him how he fared; not well (quoth he),
> An ague this two months has troubled me.
> I let him pass, and laughed to hear his 'scuse:

> For I knew well, he had the pox by *Luce*,
> And wore his night-cap ribboned at the ears,
> Because of late he sweat away his hairs.

'Luce' would have been Luce Morgan, once a maid of honour at Court, who ended up in a brothel in Clerkenwell.

Some people tried tobacco, thought of as health-giving, or mineral waters at Bath. Another treatment was guiac, or guiacum, derived from a wood used by Amazon tribesmen. It was introduced to Europe in 1523 by the humanist scholar Ulrich von Hutten, in his 1519 book *De guaiaci medicina et morbo gallico*. Black in colour, it was confused with ebony; whilst tried as a (less toxic) treatment it was also thought of as poisonous in itself: Hamlet's poisoned father's ghost refers to 'cursed ebona', presumably meaning guiac. There are frequent references to the disease, its symptoms and treatment, in Shakespeare – most obviously to Falstaff's condition in *Henry IV, Part Two*; Mistress Quickly, owner of the bawdy house who helped give it him, dies of 'the malady of France', as Pistol reports in *Henry V*. In *Timon of Athens*, misanthropic Timon vindictively urges two whores to infect others:

> Give them diseases, leaving with thee their lust … .
> Consumptions sow in hollow bones of men … .
> … Down with the nose,
> Down with it flat, take the bridge quite away …
> Make civil-pated ruffians bald … . Plague all,
> That your activity may defeat and quell
> The source of all erection.

In *Troilus and Cressida* Thersites mentions another symptom, 'the Neapolitan bone-ache ... the curse depending on those that war for a placket.'

What was taken for syphilis was, in fact, often gonorrhea, itself thought of as the precursor of 'the great pox'. Burning pain in urination was also widely reported, and even figures in Shakespeare's later sonnets associated with the so-called 'Dark Lady', especially towards the end, where the conventional fire of love is conflated with the fire of disease, and where he hopes for a 'seething bath' to cure 'strong maladies'.

There, chaste Diana's maid can quench the burning, and Cupid, with 'a cool well … . Which from Love's fire took heat perpetual, / Growing a bath and healthful remedy / For men diseased.'

Turning from these distresses at the end of the sequence, Shakespeare remembered a verse from Chapter Eight of the Bible's 'Song of Solomon', how, 'Many waters cannot quench love', and concluded with significant ambiguity, that 'Love's fire heats water, water cools not love' – which itself makes for a happier conclusion here.

Chapter 2

Men About Town

Two Elizabethan men, Simon Forman[1] and Thomas Whythorne,[2] wrote journals of their lives that present very different pictures of sexual activity in London at the time. One is a story of severe moral restraint and inhibition while the other is an account of an unusually varied and energetic sexual life – by any standards – without any regard for conventional morality. Simon Forman was the notorious and celebrated astrological physician, whose career furnishes illuminating, and occasionally surprising, views of the real sex lives of at least some Elizabethans.

Born on 31 December 1552 (as an astrologer he was fussy about exact dates and times), near Wilton in Wiltshire and of modest origins, Forman was educated at grammar school in Salisbury, but was apprenticed to a grocer or general dealer on his father's death in 1563. He taught briefly at a school in Wilton, before going to Oxford in attendance upon two better off but idle cousins. Here he picked up some education, but left Magdalen College as only a *literatus* – one who had attended but without a degree. He went back to teaching at Wilton and when the Queen visited the Earl and Countess of Pembroke in 1574, he was chosen to deliver a welcoming oration (in Latin). In 1579, he settled near Salisbury to 'practise physic and magic', and decided to become a physician, and read Galen and other medical books, as well as astrology (horoscopes were frequently used as help in diagnosis). However, to practise, he needed a licence from the College of Physicians, which was never forthcoming, and the lack of which caused him considerable difficulties throughout his career. In 1579 and 1581, he was imprisoned at Salisbury for practising medicine without a licence.

In 1582 he met his first love, Anne Young (referred to as A. Y. in his autobiography). She was the daughter of 'a man of good reputation and wealth', who would not have looked kindly on Simon, of no background, money or even good looks (he was short and gingery). He writes that she

> loved Simon [he often referred to himself in the third
> person] wonderfully well, and would surely see him once a
> day, or else she would be sick. As for Simon, he loved her
> not but in kindness, but because she was so kind to Simon,
> he would do any thing he could for her. And this love on her
> side lasted long, as hereafter shall be showed.

Despite this, it was later that year, with someone else, that his active sex life began, at the age of 29, when he records (using the curious code word 'halek' that he invented): 'this was the first year in sum that ever I did halek cum mujer [Spanish for woman].'

He earned a little by tutoring and practising medicine of sorts, so that in February 1583 he 'did halek cum two women … we went to London and lay there until we had spent all.'

Soon after this he met up with Anne again, initially as her doctor, but '29 February [1584] was the first time that ever I did halekekeros harescum A. Y.' She was probably married by this time (in her mid-twenties); on 27 March 1585 she bore a son, known as Joshua Walworth, the son of Ralph Walworth. Nevertheless, her affair with Simon continued. He records that on 1 January 1587 he and A. Y. 'were like to have been betrayed', and in November 1588 'the constable came for A. Y. and there followed much sorrow after it.' Presumably, they had been denounced to the Church court for adultery. It was as well that in August 1589 he set off for London.

In March 1590 he was able to take a lease on a house in Billingsgate, just east of London Bridge, a busy trading centre which was convenient for city merchants' families and sailors and their families from the dock areas. Most of his clients were women, asking about possible pregnancies, difficulties with menstruation, and – as an astrologer, he had also taken up necromancy (communicating with the dead), invoking spirits 'from the vasty deep' – what might happen to their husbands, especially the sailors. Male clients tended to have worries about their genitals, or whether their wives were faithful.

About that time he met a young woman in the street, whom he fancied. He made enquiries about her family, and went round to her house; the parents were out, but she and a friend made him welcome. He sent out for a quart of wine, things went well, and another possible suitor was sent away. When the mother returned, she also made him welcome, and gave him a meal of gammon and cheese with the father. At 6 pm, after two kisses, he went home, and matters looked very promising, until he did an astrological cast of her, which indicated that 'she would prove a whore and bear outward in her appearance a fair show, but she will play the whore privily.' And that was the end of that.

More important matters now intervened: the return of bubonic plague in 1592 and 1594 had a disastrous effect; in 1593 10,675 Londoners died. Those with money, including not only the senior clergy and parish priests but many of the physicians, got out of town and went to the country. However, Simon stayed, and worked for his people. He himself found swellings around his genitals; they could well have been venereal sores, but when 'the red tokens as broad as halfpence' also appeared on his feet, he decided they were plague sores. He treated the disease, whatever it was, by lancing the buboes and drinking a medical concoction of his own devising. It worked, and his treatment made his name locally. 'I began to be known and came to credit,' he recorded, before adding one of the little doggerel verses he enjoyed:

> And in the time of Pestilent Plague,
> When Doctors all did fly
> And got them into places far
> From out the City,
> The Lord appointed me to stay
> To cure the sick and sore,
> But not the rich and mighty ones
> But the distressed poor.

Afterwards he published a pamphlet, *A Discourse of the Plague, written by Simon Forman, practising physician and astrologer, 1593.*

In the same year he was consulted by Alice Blague, the youthful wife of Dean Blague, Dean of Rochester, an unusual wife for a senior clergyman. Forman wrote:

> She had wit at will but was somewhat proud and wavering, given to lust and to diversity of loves and men. And did, in

lewd banqueting, gifts and apparel, consume her husband's wealth, to satisfy her own lust and pleasure and idle company. And always in love with one or another. She loved one Cox, a gentleman, on whom she spent much. After that she loved Dean Wood, a Welshman who cozened her of much; she consumed her husband for love of that man. She did much over-rule her husband. She was of long visage, wide mouth, reddish hair, of good and comely stature; but would never garter her hose and would go much slipshod. She had four boys, a maid and a shift [miscarriage].

Not surprisingly, halek took place twice that June. She consulted him frequently, and became a friend of sorts.

Also at that time he met Avisa Allen, who was to be the most important woman in his life. The wife of William Allen, of nearby Thames Street and a Catholic of about 32, she is described as 'somewhat tall, a good motherly face, fair and of a good nature and disposition'. He went on: 'She was friendly faithful to the end but there was many breaks between us.' It is clear that, despite her sense of guilt and his infidelities, this was a real love relationship, strongly sexual but troubled by their intense mutual jealousy and quarrels. She first consulted him as a doctor early in November; on 29 November, at 3 pm, 'Avisa Allen and I first osculavimus [kissed]', and on 15 December, 'halek Avisa Allen primus'. The affair took off, while he became a friend of both Allens.

Nonetheless, quarrels soon began, as Avisa was jealous of one Joan Wild. She broke off sexual relations with Forman in April, but was reconciled on 9 December. (It was actually Alice Barker she should have been jealous of, in February and March 1595.) On 7 June he had halek with Avisa, who, however, was infuriated to find Joan Wild waiting for him, and broke off with him again, only to manage halek once more two weeks later, in a private town garden. The puritanical but prurient Philip Stubbes, who disapproved of most things, wrote in *The Anatomy of Abuses* (1583) that:

> In the fields and suburbs of the cities they have gardens, either paled or walled around very high, with their arbours and bowers fit for the purpose … . And for that their gardens are locked, some of them have three or four keys

a-piece, whereof one they keep for themselves, the other
their paramours have to go in before them, lest haply they
should be perceived, for then were all their sport dashed ... .
These gardens are excellent places, and for the purpose; for
if they can speak with their darlings nowhere else, yet there
they may be sure to meet them and to receive the guerdon
[reward] of their pains; they know best what I mean.

About this time, Forman even rode down to Wilton and broke off with
Anne Young. Back in London, the combination of frequent halek and
Avisa's guilt (about adultery, and as a Catholic) continued; in September
1595 Avisa became pregnant. She asked Simon whether she should
consult Dr Stanhope, who dealt with recusant Catholics, but he advised
her not to. Halek continued, either at home or in the garden. (Meanwhile,
it appears that he had fathered another child. On 11 March, he noted
that Alice Barker was pregnant, and she sent for him the next day; 'the
21st day I was before the Bench of Aldermen for Alice Barker,' when
presumably he had to acknowledge fathering a child and promise to
maintain it. On 20 April, he wrote that Anne was christened.)

In September, Avisa's husband, William, was very ill, near death; his
death would have enabled them to marry, but he recovered. The College
of Physicians continued to pursue Forman over his lack of qualifications,
and he was again fined – £10 – and imprisoned briefly in Counter Prison
in Wood Street. They were after him again in September 1596, and he
was in the Counter for two weeks. Further jealous spats broke out, with
Avisa jealous of her servant, Kate, with Forman, and Forman of his
servant, William, with Avisa, but they were reconciled again and shortly
after Christmas they 'halekekeros cum tauro'.

All this while he was exploiting his opportunities with his women
clients. In January 1596, there was halek with Julian Clark in Seething
Lane, and then with Margaret App, followed by Julian a week
later; and on 28 February, halek with Anne Nurse at 3 pm, 'Ankers' at
6 pm, and Judith, who stayed overnight. On 2 March he was with Joan
West, and then with Avisa in her garden on 12 March, and then with
Elizabeth Hipwell, wife of 'a lewd fellow ... spends all he gets, keeps
bad company'; she had a bad reputation also.

On 26 June, Avisa gave birth to Alexander Allen; Simon cast the
child's horoscope which was not good, and the baby died soon after.

This caused Avisa great grief and guilt; her horoscope indicated that 'she desireth much of Venus', presumably as a reassurance. Her health remained bad, and on 6 June she sent urgently for Simon and four days later William himself came round and brought him to her, but there was little that he could do. On 21 June, he recorded, simply, 'Avisa Allen died.' At this point, there was nothing else to say. She was undoubtedly the most intense emotional experience of his life.

His casebooks recorded the various sex lives and problems of his clients, both lower class and gentry. Avisa's servant, Kate, was pregnant by her lover, Robert Barnes, whom Simon treated for 'gonorrhoea passio and smarting of his urine'. He recorded how one Clemence Scarborough 'came by chance into a house where a fellow came a-wooing to a widow. He left off the widow, and fell in with an old woman and persuaded her to marry him.' The man then sold all she had, and married Clemence, bigamously, before leaving her to fend for herself for five years. Meanwhile, she married another man with a yellow beard. The first man came back, sued for divorce, sold all she had and left her again, in misery, at 25, with four children. She 'then was a meretrix [whore], glad to shift for herself. She was a little black woman. He used the sea much as a soldier and captain, and would consume all.'

Another marriage that could not have gone well, and is a sad story, was that of Mary Best. Wrote Forman:

> The same night that Mary Best was married she came to John Coles's bedside and told him she should be married the morning following. He took her into bed and did halek. Now at Shrovetide last, when he went to sea, he and one Laurence and company went to a tavern in Bishopgate Street and were there all day. And Mary sent Cole a bracelet of her hair with her name therein.

Poor unhappy Mary.

On 17 May 1597, Forman was consulted by Emilia Lanier (née Bassano), aged 27, a poet, former Court musician and then mistress of Lord Hunsdon, the Lord Chamberlain. When she had become pregnant in 1593, she had been married off to Alphonse Lanier, a French Court musician. Simon describes her as having been maintained well, and that she had been 'brave [fashionable] in youth. She hath many false conceptions.

She hath a son, his name is Henry' (after his father). She originally consulted Forman in his astrological capacity, wishing to know whether Lanier would gain a promotion – even a knighthood – after the Islands Voyage to the Azores. On 2 September she asked if she might also get a title of some sort, as she 'hath been favoured much of her Majesty and of many noblemen ... but her husband hath dealt hardly with her, hath spent and consumed her goods. She is now very needy, in debt, and it seems for lucre's sake will be a good fellow, for necessity doth compel.' His horoscope of her suggested 'she hath a mind to the queynt [sex], but she is or will be a harlot ... she useth sodomy' (possibly as a contraceptive method). On 11 September he went round to her, when 'she would not halek. Yet he felt all parts of her body willingly and kissed her often, but she would not do in any wise.' Nevertheless, on 17 September she sent for him, and again on 23 September, for halek.

His sexual career continued, with varying success. On one occasion he visited Isabella Webb while her husband was downstairs, kissing and touching her, but, not surprisingly, that was as far as she would go at that time. In October, he struck lucky, sexually, when he went to see the State Opening of Parliament by the Queen. In the crowd, 'a gentlewoman stood by him to whom he promised some courtesy, and in conference on further matters to come to him at any time if he did send to her. He sent his man round to her at 4 p.m., and she came presently, and did halek very friendly.' This instance of casual sex sought out by a middle-class woman seems to be an example of the kind of activity complained of at the time by the professionals, which suggests that it was not infrequent in London. In Ben Jonson's play, *Bartholomew Fair* (1614), the 'punk of Turnbull [Lane], ramping Alice', berates, not without cause, Judge Overdo's wife:

> A mischief on you, they are such as you are, that undo us,
> and take our trade from us, with your tuft-taffeta haunches
> [fancy-padded behinds] ... . The poor common whores can
> ha' no traffic for the privy rich ones; your caps and hoods
> of velvet cull away our customers, and lick the fat from us.

After his casual encounter, Forman went round to Emilia Lanier and stayed all night. It is not clear how frequently they met, but the relationship ended in 1600.

Her way of life changed after this, as she made up to important Court ladies, notably the Countess of Suffolk, and in 1611 she published a long religious poem, *Salve Deus Rex Judaeorum*, about the virtues of the women of the Bible, from Eve to Jezebel, which would have gone down well with the sisterhood. She outlived her husband, and died in April 1654. On the basis of her connection with Hunsdon (patron of Shakespeare's theatre company), her musicality and sexuality, historian A. L. Rowse suggested her as the model for Shakespeare's 'Dark Lady of the Sonnets', a suggestion that has not generally found favour.

Forman was always alert for halek opportunities. For example, he haleked Ann Sedgwick 'alias Catlyn' in Aldersgate Street, 'right up against the Cock', shortly after seeing the play, *Sir John Oldcastle* (a spin-off from Shakespeare's *Henry IV*), at the Rose theatre, but he was also still looking for a possible wife. In September, he thought the widow Calverley of Holborn might do, or Mistress Withypoll, whom he encountered at Stourbridge Fair, who caught his attention as she was 'much like Avis Allen, for whose sake I now have a good affection for her.' He tried for the widow Boothby, but got nowhere, nor with Katherine Gittens and Sarah Archdell, whom he met at the Curtain theatre. (Theatres had become good pick-up places, as the puritans observed; thus Stephen Gosson, in *The Schoole of Abuse* in 1579: 'In our assemblies at plays in London, you shall see such heaving and shoving, such itching and shouldering, to sit by women ... such toying, such smiling, such winking and such manning them home when the sports are ended, that it is a right comedy to mark their behaviour.')

Among his regular clients were John and Anne Condwell, whom he met in October 1598; he treated him for stone and gravel and she asked if she were pregnant. On 16 January 1601, he had halek with Anne at 9 am, and at noon that day with Frances Hill, her maidservant; Anne was to become one of his regular suppliers of halek. That year, 1598, also saw the beginning of a troublesome relationship when he hired Elizabeth Parker as a housekeeper and nurse (presumably with his women clients in mind), and haleked her on 14 July '*et eo tempore fugit matrix virgam virilem*', that is, taking her virginity; and had halek twice again four days later. He carried on with her for some time; early in November she wondered if she was pregnant. Later that month, his step-nephew, Stephen Mitchell, came to stay, and Simon found her 'on the bed, kissing with him and the boys, I being then abed'; Simon joined them 'until almost eleven at night'. Soon after, he reclaimed solitary possession, and 'halek E. Parker 9.15 p.m. *et seminavi per multum semen et matrix hausit multum tempusque'*. Despite this performance, in December she left his service, and soon after that informed him that she was pregnant.

In March 1599, Elizabeth's brothers came round, wanting to know who dunnit, and what was he going to do. Forman told them about the fun and games with Mitchell, and how, before that, on 22 August, she had been sent 'to Mary Fardell that lay in childbed and Nicholas Fardell did occupy her before she came away.' The brothers were not persuaded, and legal action for maintenance began. Forman prepared notes for the defence:

> Remember these that follow Whitfield, how he had her.
> That the smith used her. Captain Ruddlesdon at Mr Bragg's.
> Fardell of Southwark when I sent her to his wife's lying-in.
> The time that she went to Hackney and she went not thither
> but to Lambeth. The time that she went to Fleet Street, when
> I went to Lambeth in an afternoon and forbade her to go out.
> The time she stayed so long at market.

However accurate this list may have been, it was not enough, and, before the matter reached court, he agreed to pay money for her nurse and the man who was persuaded to marry her before the child was born on 9 June (when Forman insisted, in vain, that the dates were right for Fardell to be the father).

Forman was a hard worker, and successful (which is why, perhaps, the Parkers had latched onto him). On 20 February, he took six cases, on 22 February, five, on the 23rd, seven, on the next day, five. He cast horoscopes, diagnosed, prescribed, treated, even did a little surgery – scrofula, stomach pains, ulcers, fevers, rheumatic problems, pregnancies, venereal infections – besides being busy with astrology, alchemy and trying his hand at necromancy. (The Queen's astrologer, the famous John Dee, practised necromancy, as did Shakespeare's Prospero.) Around the turn of the century, he acquired more salubrious surroundings in Lambeth.

On 22 July 1599, at the age of 47, he married. His wife, Jane Baker, aged 17 or 18, was the daughter of John Baker of Canterbury, late proctor in the Church court. How it came about is not clear. Later, he wrote, 'he married her at Lambeth by chance asking her a question in that behalf, the which she took advantage of, and he would not go from his word.' A careless word of promise in front of a witness, and he was snapped up. It could happen to anyone (as Whythorne was to fear). In *The Taming of the Shrew* (IV.4), Biondello jested, 'I knew a wench married in an afternoon as she went to the garden for parsley to stuff a rabbit.' There is no mention of a dowry; her chief asset was her uncle, Sir Edward Munnings, a connection Forman valued, especially as it linked him with gentry. The wedding took place on Sunday, at 7 am, at Lambeth Parish Church, and he recorded, 'I was married to Anne Baker of Kent.' Who? Presumably this was actually Jane, here confused with his first love, Anne Young. It was a small gathering. Among those present were 'friend Condwell', Simon's man, John Braddedge, the bride's mother and her man, and 'one Fratell', who gave the bride away. Simon paid the curate eight shillings and two pence; his bed friend, Mrs Blague, helped with the occasion, when 'they dined at Mrs Blague's, and came home between 1 and 2 p.m.'

Their sex life was prompt and active, though she was young and her first period did not take place until 3 October 1600. He does not appear to have particularly cared for her: 'I married her, she had nothing in respect to take to, and she was somewhat choleric of nature and self-willed yet quickly rebuked at last.' From the first he was anxious about her fidelity; the horoscope in September suggested 'she will be meretrix for it seems policy'. He himself was busy with Jane's maid, Frances Hill, as well as Anne Condwell. On 9 April, after Jane had lied about where she had been when he was at the Royal Exchange, there was a fierce quarrel when:

> Because I liked not her lies and excuses she began to talk
> peremptory with me, howling and weeping, and would not
> be quiet till I gave her two or three boxes [round the head].
> She upbraids me with her friends. It seems that she will be a
> whore and went out with some other intent. But as yet there
> is no fact done.

Such a beating would not have been considered remarkable or reprehensible. It was common for husbands to beat obstreperous wives (or even, on occasion, vice versa), and couples would frequently beat children or servants. (Even the Queen boxed the ears of the Earl of Essex in 1599.) Early in 1600, he was boasting of how well he was doing financially, and spending £40 on himself and £50 on his wife on clothes alone. He mentions his new purple gown, velvet cap, coat, breeches and taffeta cloak. He let his hair and beard grow, and had his portrait painted.

For all his concern about his wife's fidelity, Forman continued his own multiple halek activities. On 15 January 1605, he records halek with Anne Condwell at 9 am and Frances Hill at noon. On 8 June 1607, Hester Sharpe was at 9 am, Anne Documan at 3 pm and his wife (now nicknamed 'Tronco') at 9 pm. It does seem impressive for a man of 55. No doubt there were others, unrecorded. His journal ends in 1602, with just a few notes after that.

The unmarried twentieth-century historian A. L. Rowse writes, 'However, married life set in with its usual severity' – though Forman's married life was unlikely to be 'usual'. On 27 October 1606, his wife gave birth at home to their first son, Clement, in the midst of a particularly virulent outbreak of the plague. His neighbours, suspecting him of harbouring plague in the household, 'railed on him and his wife, being but two hours before delivered'. They barricaded him, his family and servants inside the house, saying it would be better for them to starve than for any of them to be put in danger. He wrote, 'The great injury the Lambithians did to me and my wife shall rest in record until the day of doom.' What particularly hurt was that these people included some that he had treated: 'I did not then shut up my compassion from any nor my doors, as they have done to me.'

Notwithstanding the continued persecution by the College of Physicians, he continued to practise and do well, becoming quite well off, and in 1603 was licensed to practise by Cambridge University. He was respectable enough to be on the fringes of the Court, ministering to the various needs of Court ladies. Early in 1610 he was consulted by Anne Turner, wife of Dr George Turner and mistress of Sir Arthur Mainwaring. When her husband died, she wanted Forman to give her a potion to make Mainwaring marry her; he agreed but despite its potency, Mainwaring did not ask for her hand.

Anne Turner later approached him again, not for herself, but on behalf of Frances Howard, unhappily married to Robert, third Earl of Essex but in love with Robert Carr, a favourite of King James. The proposal was that he should supply potions to make Essex impotent, and ensure Carr's desire for her. During 1611 Frances wrote frequently to Forman, addressing him as 'father': 'Sweet Father, I must still needs crave your love, though I hope I shall have it', and again: 'I hope you will do me good ... . Remember me, for God's sake, and get me from this vile place. – Your assured, affectionate, loving daughter, Frances Essex.'

It is not clear just how far Simon was involved in this dreadful business, that eventually led to the murder of Thomas Overbury, with Howard and Carr accused. According to a later astrologer/physician, William Lylly, Forman prophesied his own death, in September 1611. He was 59.

* * * * *

The other autobiographer, Thomas Whythorne, could hardly be more different, showing an unusual degree of caution and restraint when it came to relationships with women. This was derived partly from a strong moral – even puritanical – sense, and apparently from an inbuilt sexual inhibition. Born in Somerset in 1528, he was what one might call middle class; a trained musician who made his living as a music tutor to gentleman-class families, especially women. In his autobiography he describes himself as always careful of 'the allurements, enticements and snares of women'. It seems that sometime in his youth, some psychological damage had been done him. Despite this, he appears to have been attracted and attractive to several women. He also seems to have shared the common suspicion of women's sexuality: 'Though they be weaker vessels, yet they will overcome 2, 3 or 4 men in the satisfying of their carnal appetites.'

He came to London in 1545, aged 17. Early in his career he was living as a music tutor to a family where the young maidservant of the household developed a crush on him, writing him little love notes. However, 'this matter coming to her master and mistress's knowledge, and finding that she was so loving without provoking or enticing thereto, she was discharged out of that house and service.' Even though employers at the time felt responsible for the conduct and morals of their employees, this seems severe. It might, however, have been a kindness to her in the long run, and a relief to the general atmosphere in the household, being spared hopeless yearning and moping.

Things might have been much worse: there was a case (not mentioned in his memoir) where a tutor, Allen Carr, was accused of impregnating his employers' maid, Ellen Vaughan, which he denied. Her employers – unusually – helped her, by locking him in his room, to prevent him from getting away. Ellen was determined to have him: as she later admitted, she believed that 'with a loud voice weeping and crying aloud … she would cause the same Carr to be hanged although she were hanged with him unless he would marry her.' Her employer, Richard Philips, told Carr – through the window – that he should marry her. 'Well,' quoth the same Carr, 'if I be forced thus to marry her, I assure you she shall never enjoy good day with me, for I hate her.' The next day, the priest was brought, the door unlocked and the ceremony executed. Carr 'utterly refused' to consummate the marriage. When he sued for separation on the grounds of an enforced marriage, the Philips spoke in his favour, as there was no evidence of a child, and he was released. Ellen lost her job, and was punished.[3]

After what might have been a narrow escape, young Thomas then became music tutor and some kind of servant or page to a gentleman's widow, who liked to have men wooing her, and made up to him, but only out of vanity, to encourage him. He wrote:

> Many times when I was not nigh her, although she had appointed me to wait on her cup when she sat at meat, she would bid me come nigher unto her. And therewith scoffingly she would say to those that were near her, 'I would fain have my man to be in love with me, for then he would not be thus far from me, but would always be at mine elbow.' When she would say that she would fain have me in love with her, these words would offend me very much, for, of all things, I accounted loving as she meant it to be but a foolish thing in those days, being in dotage, that is to say, nothing beloved again.

The widow played him for some time, trying to catch him with some commitment that she could then exploit. She would flirt, and even give him little presents, such as rings, and he would go along with this, while the job lasted. He continued:

> Marry, thus much may I say, that I, being loth that she should withdraw her good will from me, was very serviceable to

please her; and also would sometimes be pleasant and merry, and also somewhat bold with her. After the which times, she would sometimes tell me in a scoffing manner that I was but a huddypick [simpleton], and lacked audacity. But I, not construing those words so then, as they did proceed from one who did know her game, or else had learned that, as he that wooeth a maid must be brave in apparel and outward show, so he that wooeth a widow must not carry quick [live] eels in his codpiece but show some proof that he is stiff before, did think her show of love and liberality bestowed upon me was but to feed her humour, and to bring her purpose to pass (as aforesaid). That is to say, to bring me in such a doting love towards her, whereby I should suffer her to ride and deride me as she list.

She wanted to keep him as a sort of plaything, or toyboy, and when he had a chance of going to a place in the household of the Duchess of Northumberland, she would not let him. Eventually, however, he got away from her clutches, and made for the open air, travelling abroad, to Flanders and Italy, presumably working as some kind of musician.

When he came back to England, he was wary of finding himself in the same position and insisted he be 'used as a friend and not as servant. Upon this [his new employers] not only allowed me to sit at their table but also of their own mess [sharing their meals].' Having grown up and ready to move on, emotionally, with a mind to marriage, he was attracted to 'a young gentlewoman who, not only for her gifts of nature was man's meat, but also for her gifts of the mind, and possibility of living [there was money in the family, though he had none], was worthy to be looked on and sued to for marriage.' He even went through the rituals of courtship, singing her love songs. However, there was the usual problem associated with moneyed young gentlewomen. Quite properly, she said:

I thank you for your good will, but I pray you be content, and speak no more unto me of your suit. For that possibility of living, which I have, is not so certain but that it dependeth wholly upon the good will and pleasure of my parents.

And therefore, if I should not be ruled by them in giving my consent in marriage, I should have nothing of them to live by hereafter.

After that, he moved on to employment in a nobleman's household, living in the family house in the country. A near neighbour was a 'mean gentleman, an ancient widower, and he had to govern his house an ancient matron and maid ... Mistress Elizabeth, likely to be his heir, as manager and bedmate.' He and the others in the household, including the family chaplain, used to visit her for 'feasts', as she was friendly and generous. When one of them complimented her, she said that she could 'keep a good house – if I had Mr Whythorne to be my husband'. They had got into the habit of toasting each other, and she said that they could then call each other husband and wife, to which he replied with good humour:

> 'I did not know your mind certainly in this matter till now. And therefore now I drink unto you, gentle wife, with all my heart.'
> 'I pledge you, good husband,' quoth she.
> 'Yea,' quoth the (chop-logic, I would have said) chaplain aforesaid, 'Be ye so soon agreed?'
> 'Come on,' quoth he, 'and I'se make ye sure, that shall I.'
> (He spake the words northernly, because he was a northern man.) And with those [words], he took her by the hand and reached to have taken mine also. [This was a moment of real danger of entrapment for Thomas, with words spoken before a priest.]
> 'No, soft,' quoth I, to the chaplain. 'Soft fire maketh sweet malt. Nay, I will woo a little before I be made sure. For we do see sometimes that they who do marry in haste, have time enough afterward for to repent them.'
> 'Nay,' quoth he then (and with that he did let go her hand), 'I do but mean merrily.'
> 'It may be so,' quoth I. (But for all that, I thought then that such a contract, made by a priest, and in such sort as it seemed he would have done it, might have turned some one or both of us some disquietness in the end.)

Afterwards, the others chaffed him about it:

> And then did one say to me, 'Will you marry with such a withered scroil [witch] as that is?' Quoth another, 'Will ye have such an old crooked crone as she is?' Quoth another, 'And if you have her, ye shall have no more with her than shall please her master to give with her. For he hath had the flour of her, and you shall have but the bran.'

For them to talk like this, he must have led her on in front of them. She may well have had some hopes of young Thomas, for after this episode she went into a severe decline, and he moved on again.

In his next employment he got involved in a serious emotional crisis, when genuine feeling, morality and inhibition were entangled. He became tutor to a gentleman's children in a household five miles from London. The wife was clearly a charmer, a former courtier, 'well experienced also in affairs of the world, and also she had a great wit, and a jolly, ready tongue to utter her fantasy and her mind, that I took pleasure many times to talk and discourse.' Obviously, they flirted with each other. Meanwhile, he was also tutoring another gentleman's children in London.

When he had been there a while, the first woman told him that if her husband wearied of paying him, she would pay, and that, if he left, he would always be welcome. She then said: 'And, what pleasure soever I am able to do you or for you at any time, by any manner mean whatsoever it be, if you will let me understand it, you shall be assured of it at all times.' That seems clear enough; though all she may have had in mind was a pleasant little fling, such as married ladies, especially Court ladies, often had – nothing serious, no harm done. In response, Whythorne coolly thanked her, and assured her of his regard for her. He also got the impression that his London hostess, a widow, would like to have him as a husband, but he thought, shrewdly, that not only was she past childbearing for him, but also 'he who weddeth with a widow who hath two children, he should be cumbered with three thieves; because that the mother … will purloin and filch from her husband to bestow it upon her children.' (The current proverb only warned against a widow with one child.) Doubting Thomas was always very careful (though he could have had the use of their portions until they came of age).

Back in the first household, the lady gave him an expensive New Year's Day gift, and moved his chest of clothes next to her room, which alarmed him, as he remembered, 'Thou shalt not commit adultery.' She followed up, as he recorded:

> In her house, I being in my chamber all alone, she one day took occasion to come all alone into my chamber to see the marks of my sheets. Wherewithal I began straightways to think that she did to see what kindness I would offer unto her when she was in my chamber. And that which I offered her was none other but that I suffered her to be in my chamber as long as she list without troubling her; and not once touched her all the while she was there, but suffered her to part away as quietly as she came there.

At the time, 'suffer' meant 'allow', but the modern sense also seems applicable. It must have been a tense and embarrassing time for him but worse for her, waiting for him, with the strong feeling between them remaining unacknowledged, unspoken, when what happened was that nothing happened. She left, 'quietly'. She had lost. She moved his chest back again: there was no hope.

A different pot was on the tepid boil when a friend told Whythorne that there was another wealthy woman looking to marry, which aroused his calculating interest. About this time, he was insensitive enough to tell the lady of a young woman in the household, whom he thought he might marry, and asked her opinion. Not surprisingly, she discouraged him, saying:

> The maid is my husband's kinswoman, and therefore he will bestow her where he liketh. And if you would sue to him for his will to have her, I am sure it would be such a troublesome piece of work for you as it would disquiet you very much. This much do I show you for your good will … and therefore, if you will be counselled by me, do you never proceed any further in it.

Presumably he was not of sufficient status for the husband to approve him, and she was unlikely to want this to happen. It may not have been a real proposition, but a tactic of discouragement on his part. It is no wonder that a coolness followed.

The friend now told him that

> her fallings out with me was for that I did not feed her humour and offered her more kindness than I had done (ye know what I mean). And he said that, and if I had done so, it would not only have put by all our fallings out, but also have vantaged me above forty pounds for a reward. [At least Whythorne was above that.] Then said I unto him that he was deceived in her. 'Tush, man,' quoth he, 'ye are but a novice in such cases. All is not gold that seemeth to be so, nor every one a saint that seemeth to be one. I did perceive by her face, her complexion, colour of eyes and demeanour when I was at her house, what her inclination is that way. And also I did perceive, by the entertainment that she gave, what her affection was toward you.

However, by now the lady, though in love, had given up whatever hope she had had of him. On one occasion she said that

> she would be content to give and to help an honest man and also to profit and further him, yet she did it not because that she would play the harlot with him. The which words I took to be meant towards me. And therefore I took occasion upon her words to think that whatsoever she had said towards me before that time, she meant not to do it for any dishonesty. Wherefore now I began to be merrier than I had been a long time before in her company.

He was safe. Then:

> in a time in talk of love matters, she looked me very earnestly in the face and said that they who loved where their love was not requited must, as well they might, refrain the same again. At the which words I was somewhat abashed, but yet I said nothing thereto … she said on a time if a man (peradventure she might have said a woman) who feared God, did love

otherwise than he ought, it would be a great torment to his conscience. To the which I answered that, to such a one, his body was a hell unto himself. The which words I spake then upon some experience; for I must confess that I loved her as much as I might do with a safe conscience, because that she well deserved it.

At last an admission of his hobbled feelings for her. We should assume that, consciously at least, his behaviour was motivated by a genuine religious sense and observance of the Seventh Commandment. As for 'kindness', it would have been kinder for him to leave her alone in her distress. 'She said, "The good that I would do, that do I not; but the ill which I hate, that do I." These last words she would say divers times.' She could not bring herself to love her husband as she should, but could not stop wanting Whythorne, though knowing that was wrong. Meanwhile, he even claimed to himself to have consideration for the husband's reputation, not to be known as a cuckold: 'A notorious cuckold is barred of divers functions and callings of estimation in the commonwealth, as a man defamed.' He observed that 'a man's honesty and credit doth depend and lie in his wife's tail'.

He may have been getting anxious, in case the husband became suspicious: 'It is not good for a man to search too narrowly to know the truth of his wife's folly that way.' It would be better for a husband to suppress any suspicions, let alone obtain knowledge, and keep quiet. 'For if he be known to know that his wife is a strumpet and yet doth keep her still, he shall be reputed to be not only a cuckold but also a wittol'. Conversely, 'if he do put her from him, yet thereby he denounceth himself to be a cuckold for ever after.' It would be best if Whythorne were to break off. As it was, he did at last leave.

Soon enough, his mercenary friend told him of 'a widow, one of worshipful parentage and hath twenty pounds a year dowry or jointure, who hath no child and is of years about five or six years younger than yourself.' A real bargain. There were some meetings and discussions of marriage, but nothing came of it. It seems to be a pattern with him – to engage sympathetically and then to freeze. He may not have been free emotionally after his recent experience; in any case, he resisted his friend's urging him to sleep with her first, as 'we should have provoked God's heavy displeasure and wrath, to have lighted upon us for our wickedness.' The young widow might have been willing to take a chance of a trial run; not everyone had his strict, puritanical repressions. She may have made some kind of promise, but he had not followed it up. 'She answered [the friend] that it was no such promise … she might break it again upon cause, and seeing that I took her not bianby [immediately] and dispatched the matter, she was determined never to marry.' Not him, anyway.

He went on with his musical career, teaching, performing and composing, and even had a volume of madrigals published in 1569 and 1571, when he would have been in his early forties. By 1577 he had somehow brought himself to marry – rather late in life, for those times – and died in 1596, a well-preserved 68.

Chapter 3

How to Get Married

Making a Match

When it came to getting married, there were various ways of going about it, some officially approved, and others less so. For those concerned with money and status, which was most people, marriage was a matter of negotiations and agreements with families and friends, with a view to protecting and furthering family interests. In 1606, Nicholas Breton expressed a particularly jaundiced view of the whole business, writing, 'There is no such thing [as marrying for love]; there is bargaining and selling, looking and telling, lust and folly, commanding and obeying, marrying and getting of children.' In his *Cornucopiae*[1] he complained:

> For 'tis not now in elder days,
> When marrying was contracted by affection,
> For kindred now so much the matter sways,
> The parties have small choice in love's election;
> But many times, ere one behold the other,
> An unadvised match the friends do smother,
> And howsoever they two can agree,
> Their friends have wooed, and they must married be.

In 1596, the Earl of Essex wrote to a friend, Richard Bagot:

> Being glad to do anything that might be for your son's good and preferment, I did lately write my letters unto Mr Weston and solicited a motion of marriage with Mistress Lowe, a kins[wo] man of his. The gentleman hath very willingly hearkened unto it, and the gentlewoman well accepted of the motion, and conceiveth well of your son. It remaineth that you deal fatherly with him for the better effecting of this match to his good.

The proposition – just the kind of thing Breton had in mind – was not entirely altruistic on the earl's part, who at the time was concerned with building and developing a network of support for his political ambitions.

Grand families might well push their offspring into marriage, willy-nilly, with titles, estates and money in mind. In this instance, the young couple seem to have been well disposed to the idea, but this was not always the case – as when 18-year-old Penelope Devereux protested bitterly against her marriage to 'the rich Lord Rich', even during the wedding ceremony itself. Until they legally came of age, young people were under the control of parents or guardians: so Mary Sidney, aged 16, was pushed into marrying Henry Herbert, Earl of Pembroke, aged 39, as the Sidneys needed money. Popular stories and ballads insisted that older men who married younger wives were very likely to be cuckolded, sooner or later. *A Discourse of marriage and wiving* (1615) remarked, tartly, 'He that undertakes to manage in his age what hath shaked the heart of youth, may be commended for his valour, but shall ne'er be crowned for his wisdom.'[2] In his *Brief Lives*, John Aubrey suggested that this was why the earl kept his wife away from Court and temptation.

Preservation of status for the aristocracy required both money and the selection of the right class. The courtier Philip Gawdy reported in a letter 'that my Lord of Pembroke had married my Lady Mary, and now my Lord Danvers shall marry her sister Lady Alithea … it is thought very fit and convenient that every man now should marry within his own element.'[3] Likewise, in *The Tempest*, a duke's daughter is to marry a king's son. Lower down the social scale, in *Twelfth Night*, Viola, disguised as a man, assures Lady Olivia, 'My state is well. I am a gentleman.' Preserving class distinction, Sir Toby Belch says that Olivia will not marry the count because 'She'll not marry above her degree.'

Others, however might cross social boundaries for profit, as Breton observed:

> Yet many are, who not the cause regard,
> The birth, the years, nor virtues of the mind;
> For gold is first, with greedy men preferred,
> And love is last, and liking set behind.[4]

Sir John Davies put it neatly, in his verse epigram, *Against the Nobly Descended Musaeus*:

The well-born Musaeus wedded hath of late
A butcher's daughter fat, for pounds and plate:
Which match is like a pudding, sith in that
He puts the blood, her father all the fat.

In general, marriage took place about ten years after puberty, with the women in their middle twenties, the men a little later. Among the upper classes, marriage tended to be earlier; in principle, marriage could take place at the age of 7, though it could not be consummated until 12 for girls, and 14 for boys. Often, the menarche might not occur until considerably later (as was the case with Forman's young wife). For the upper classes, early consummation was necessary to guarantee the succession. In 1589, Elizabeth Manners was, at the age of 13, married off to the second Earl of Exeter, and gave birth when she was 14 years and 5 months old.[5] Teenage girls from the middle and upper classes expected early marriage. In Henry Porter's play, *Two Angry Women of Abingdon* (1599), young Mall (Mary) reflects:

Good Lord, thought I, fifteen will ne'er be here,
For I have heard my mother say that then
Pretty maids were fit for handsome men.
Fifteen past, sixteen and seventeen too,
What, thought I, will not this husband do?
Will no man marry me?

In the case of Shakespeare's Juliet, her youth, at 13, at the time of her proposed marriage, is emphasised. Interestingly, her mother, Lady Capulet, was also married early, at about that age, to a husband who appears to have been considerably older. Normally, disparity of age in marriage was disapproved of. 'One thinks it an unseemly thing, to see a young woman matched with a man that carrieth a countenance rather to be her father than her husband, and I am persuaded that young dainty damsels go as willingly to such husbands as they would to their graves,' wrote Stephano Guazzo in his *Civile Conversation* (1580).[6] Several of Shakespeare's romantic heroines are noticeably youthful: Marina (*Pericles*), 14; Miranda (*The Tempest*), almost 15; Perdita (*The Winter's Tale*), 16. Their improbable backgrounds and circumstances made them unrealistic but sentimentally appealing as romance figures for their audiences. Elizabethans, reflecting on Romeo and Juliet's youth in their city-gentry situation, might have condemned their rash impulsiveness, disobedience, lack of respect for their families and norms of society and the almost predictable disastrous consequences for their families, and might have had a different response to the play from that of modern audiences.

For all classes, the right of parents or guardians to control marriage seemed almost unarguable. In 1578, John Stockwood's sermon declared that 'children are not to marry without the consent of their parents, in whose power and choice it lieth.'[7] Still, in 1602, a young woman in Samuel Rowlands's *Tis Merrie when Gossips Meet* acknowledges, 'Our parents' wills, you know, must be obeyed.' Rebelling children need not look for financial support from their parents. A few writers did point out the drawback to enforced marriage. George Whetstone's *Heptameron* (1582) argued for 'The office of free choice, the root or foundation of marriage, which consisteth only in the satisfaction of the fancy: for where the fancy is not pleased, all the perfections in the world cannot force love, and where the fancy delighteth, many defects are perfected, or tolerated among the married.'[8]

Away from home, young maids and apprentices were also under the control of their employers. In London, there were more men than women – perhaps 139 men to 100 women – and about forty per cent of the population was under 20 years of age, which made for a lively, if restless, society, still under the supervision of the older generation. Apprenticeships usually lasted for seven years, during which time the apprentice was not allowed to marry. If a London apprentice did marry, against the rules, he had to serve his time but lost the right to practise his trade there – a considerable disincentive. At their age, at the peak of their sexual potency, there was great frustration, and this encouraged prostitution, especially in towns, and displaced energy directed at brawling and misbehaviour. (The old shepherd in *The Winter's Tale* says: 'I would there were no age between ten and three-and-twenty ... for there is nothing in the between but getting wenches with child, wronging the ancientry, stealing, fighting.') In the country, marriage might be delayed due to waiting for a father's death, in order to inherit a cottage or workable land.

Young maidservants came to London partly to get away from labour on the land but chiefly to get married. Those who did marry were generally quite poor, with few savings and not much more than what they were wearing when they got married; they could hardly provide

much by way of a marriage portion.[9] Most of them were on the look out.
In a ballad, one announces her wish:

> Some wed for money,
>   and some wed for land;
> But I'll choose a honey,
>   Shall be a handsome young man.

She says she will be careful not to have an ill-tempered or jealous man,
but look for a tradesman:

> Let him be a tailor,
>   or a neat shoemaker,   [neat – cow's leather]
> A weaver or a baker;
> If he be neat and comely
>   my love is soon won …
> Then shall he be welcome
>   Unto pretty Nan,
> For I am delightsome
> To a handsome young man.[10]

Maidservants and poorer young men might overcome financial difficulties by
marrying widows or widowered employers, as Isabella Whitney wrote in her
Wyll and Testament (1573),[11] bequeathing Londoners what they already had:

> For maidens poor, I widowers rich
>   do leave, that oft shall dote,
> And by that means shall marry them,
>   to set the girls afloat.
> And wealthy widows will I leave
>   to help young gentlemen,
> Which when you have, in any case,
>   be courteous to them then …

Clearly, it was a common practice. Maidservants marrying widowers
might even step into their predecessors' shoes, literally, by taking over
their clothes as well as the household responsibilities. For women, long
delays might lead them to take older partners, by way of compromise.

The theoretical pathway to marriage for 'the middling sort' was for the young couple's parents to agree about the social and financial arrangements. The bride's parents were to provide her dowry or portion – money, land or other valuables – at the time of the wedding or soon after, while the groom's agreed to provide a jointure or portion that the wife was to receive if widowed, and to specify her living allowance. In *The Taming of the Shrew*, Petruchio is characteristically blunt: 'I come to wive it wealthily in Padua; / If wealthily then happily in Padua.' His intended father-in-law has two daughters to dispose of (or sell). Petruchio asks, 'If I get your daughter's love, / What dowry shall I have with her to wife?' Baptista replies, 'After my death, the one half of all my lands, /And in possession, twenty thousand crowns.' Petruchio: 'And for that dowry, I'll assure her of / Her widowhood, be it that she survives me, / In all my lands and leases whatsoever. / Let specialties be therefore drawn between us, / That covenants may be kept on either hand.' He goes on to tell her:

> Your father hath consented
> That you shall be my wife; your dowry 'greed on,
> And will you, nill you, I will marry you.

The provision of the dowry could be a strain on the bride's family finances, while the receipt of the dowry could considerably benefit the groom's family. Whilst this was a crucial stage for most people, in *Twelfth Night*, Sir Toby Belch declares that he would marry Olivia's woman, Maria, with no dowry, for just 'such another jest' (as that played on Malvolio), and Sir Walter Raleigh got no dowry when he eloped with Elizabeth Throckmorton. In *King Lear*, Lear angrily tells Cordelia, 'Thy truth then be thy dower'; her startled suitors had been expecting at least a share in the kingdom. Burgundy admits, 'election makes not up on such conditions'; France takes her on spec, but later he and Cordelia return to claim their rights.

If negotiations were satisfactory, the couple could proceed to a spousal ceremony; a promise to marry, signified with the exchange of presents, usually rings (like a modern engagement). Whilst this was a commitment, it had no legal, binding force, and such gifts could be misconstrued or even denied. In one instance of the breaking off of a middle-class couple's contract, that was taken to court, a woman who had acted as a go-between said that she was entreated by Agnes Newbie to go an errand for her to James Handley, to signify her commendations verbally to him and to deliver him a ring of silver and a race [root] of ginger, of which she had bit off a piece, willing [her] to tell him that for her sake it would content him to bite off another piece of the same again.

In return, James sent her four apples, which were 'very kindly received'. Two French gold coins, an enamelled gold ring and a packet of Agnes's hair also passed between them, leading him to believe, not unreasonably, that Agnes was willing to marry him. However, it appeared that Agnes had changed her mind.[12]

People often used friends or relatives as go-betweens, to sound out the feelings or suitability of the other party. In this case, the go-between had been helpful, but the practice could be risky, as a verse suggests:

> If that thy friend do lack a little wit,
> And in his humour frame an idle fit
> To take a wife, and use thee for his wooing,
> Speak for thy friend, but for thy self be doing:
> If thou find'st her worth the catching, take her,
> If not, let thy friend be sure to have her.[13]

Such go-between practices are common in Shakespeare, in the comedies *Much Ado About Nothing* and *Twelfth Night*, and in the tragedy, *Othello*, where Iago acts the part for his own purposes.

Broken espousal contracts were fairly common. In 1574, Susanna Cole admitted to the Church court in making an espousal contract with John Rhodes under a window in her father's house in Hounslow, and told about his presents:

> Before the said contract was made she received of John Rhodes two pairs of gloves in the way of matrimony, upon talk that was between them. And after the foresaid contract so made, she received of him one purse, one pair of hose and 11 shillings and four pence in money ... thereupon she taketh herself to be assured to the said John Rhodes, and they to be man and wife together.

53

But it was not to be.[14]

Such arrangements fell through for a variety of reasons, sometimes in surprising ways. Anthony Mitchell, sexton of St James Garlickhithe in 1592, reported to the Court how he had tried to bring together Elizabeth Spakeman and Tide Clear. He quoted Clear:

> 'I' faith ... if she hath so much money as she saith she hath, I will marry her ... . She saith she hath £20, and if she will by and by or within these 5 days give me £10, let her bring her clothes and come to me when she will, and I will marry her and make her my wife.'

> 'Tush,' quoth [Mitchell], 'We will have a match of it before we go', and wished the said Clear to be contracted with [her], but he would not, and still stuck upon the money, and then [Mitchell] called his boy and willed him to take a note of their names that they might be asked in the Church the Sunday following ... . But Clear said, 'Well, do what you will, I will consent to nothing except I have the money first.' Then [Mitchell] asked her two days later if she had the money; she said, 'No ... for if he like the money better than he like me, let him go where he list.'[15]

* * * * *

Marriage Contracts

Spousal ceremonies were often regarded as equivalent to marriage and not only by the lower orders. There were two main kinds of espousal: *in verbis de future* and *in verbis de praesenti*. If the words 'I take thee', were spoken in the future tense, they only suggested a future intention, and were not binding, whereas if the present tense were used, this was a definite commitment, and binding – especially if followed by sexual intercourse. Both Church and State recognised this match as valid, even though it preceded any actual marriage ceremony. In *Twelfth Night*, Olivia and Viola/Cesario have apparently performed orally such 'a contract of eternal love' in the presence of a priest; in *As You Like It* Rosalind nearly draws Orlando into a *verba de praesenti* ceremony (which would have been invalidated, as deception). As the duchess says, in John Webster's *The Duchess of Malfi* (1613–14), 'I have heard lawyers say, a contract in a chamber / *Per verba de praesenti* is absolute marriage.'

Couples sometimes acted on this assumption. One Church court records that following one such ceremony, 'after the words of matrimony or contract matrimonial above, the said Robert and Jane were *solus cum sola* [alone] together in a chamber or convenient place by the space of two or three hours where they did ratify, confirm and consummate the said matrimony by carnal copulation.' Another man took decisive action in this spirit:

> Charles Nuttall came into the house of one Elizabeth Nuttall, widow, in Rossendale, and finding the said dorothy Nuttall in bed ... called to one to pull off his boots and said he would go to bed to his wife ... in confirmation of this former contract ... and then and there did he lie with the said dorothy and knew her carnally.[16]

Sometimes such actions could have unfortunate or predictable consequences, with pregnant brides appearing before Church courts. (Statistics suggest that this happened more in the richer south west than in the north, where Catholicism was stronger – Catholics could not marry in the Church of England.) Here is just one example of how a delay could cause problems:

> Robert Gray of Coggeshall, Essex, and his wife were contracted in the presence of their parents half a year before they were married in the face of the church. After the same contract their parents did vary in some points touching their marriage [dowries or jointures, presumably], the solemnization was deferred longer than they did expect, whereby they forgetting themselves had carnal knowledge, whereby his wife was begotten with child, desiring the judge in justice to consider of his cause.[17]

Isabella Whitney referred to younger men marrying widows: a widow could be an attractive proposition, financially, with her jointure and dower and ready money (perhaps even with a going business or other property)

55

available to transfer to her new husband. As Breton remarked in *An Olde Mans Lessons* (1605)[18]: 'Many get it by an old blind widow, that have wit to spend it with a sweeter creature.' Widows might not be old and blind: 'London widows remarried early and often in the late sixteenth and early seventeenth centuries.'[19] Whilst in the country marriages might last as long as twenty years, in unhealthy London the mean duration of marriage was around twelve years. Widows of prosperous citizens could pick and choose, so that some young bachelors – court hangers-on, fretful younger sons – might be keen to snap them up.

As it was, most widows under the age of 40 married younger men. Older second husbands were not generally attractive options, especially if they had children of their own. One ballad says:

> Shall I wed an aged man,
> That groaneth with the gout,
> And lead my life in misery,
> Within doors and without?
> No! I will have a bachelor,
> Of lively blood and bone,
> To cheer me in my latter days
> Or else I will have none.

The promise was, that

> If I take a young man,
> Although his wealth be small,
> If that he use me honestly,
> He shall be lord of all. [20]

For the men, there were thought to be drawbacks to marrying a richer widow, as William Gouge wrote: 'If a rich woman marry a poor man, she will look to be the master, and to rule him; so as the order which God hath established will be clean perverted: and the honour of marriage laid in the dust.'[21] Samuel Rowlands provided the warning: [22]

> His name of John is turned into Jack,
> She tells him, that her money clothes his back;
> And that he was a needy rascal knave,

And she hath made a man of such a slave.
Her words (last week) of love, sweetheart, and joy,
Are turned to villain, rogue and beardless boy.

One play that made much of widows remarrying was Thomas Middleton's *No Wit Like a Woman's* (1611), a city comedy concerned with competing schemes to divert a rich widow's remarriage money into one pocket or another. It contains an extraordinary attack on widows' sexuality, where a character complains how the fire of true love has now been

> corrupted by the upstart fires
> Of avarice, luxury, and inconstant heats
> Struck from the bloods of cunning clap-fall'n daughters,
> Night-walking wives, but most, libidinous widows ...

Much is made of the idea that

> Rich widows, that were wont to choose by gravity
> Their second husbands, not by tricks of blood,
> Are now so taken with loose Aretine flames
> Of nimble wantonness, and high-fed pride,
> They marry now but the third part of husbands,
> Boys, smooth-faced catamites, to fulfil their bed,
> As if a woman should a woman wed.

This last line points to what actually happens in the play, as a young woman, seeking restitution from the widow of a fraudulent businessman, dresses as a young man to woo the widow, who falls in love with her. They are wed, but not bedded, as the fake marriage is dissolved and the young woman gets her money as a dowry. At the end, the two are still emotionally involved, while the play exploits the ambiguity of cross-gender casting, with a boy playing a woman playing a boy attracting a woman played by a boy. Both male and female homosexual feelings are hinted at, as they were in several cross-dressing comedies around the turn of the century.

* * * * *

57

Courting and Caught

There was more than one way of getting someone to marry, such as seduction, or even entrapment – usually of men by women. For example. Henry Packer told the Church court how

> a little after Easter [the widow Dore of Cranham], her husband being dead and she lying alone, she persuaded him to lie in her house, and the night she lay in one bed and he in another [in the one room], and in the night she sithed [sighed] and he asked her what she ailed, and she said her feet were cold, and she willed him to come to her bed.

A more serious incident occurred in 1588, when, said John Okeden,

> Being overtaken with drink, he laid down in his clothes upon his bed; and being asleep, she [Katherine, his woman servant], by the direction of one John Wainewright came and did lie on his bed by him to the intent he should marry his maid, and they were found both together; yet by virtue of his oath he never had the knowledge of her body.

At first he was put in the stocks, but later the court discharged him.[23]

Young women servants often had difficulties with seductions by employers or fellow servants. If made pregnant, they often had to go back home, or find some other solution. Dionise Halfhead and John Walker were fellow servants in the household of Sir Lionel Cranfield, where John claimed that Dionise had seduced him when he had had too much to drink. When she became pregnant, she told him that he was responsible, and he promised to pay her expenses. He paid her four pounds – a substantial amount for a young servant – but she pursued him and sued him for marriage; however, as an apprentice he could not marry and needed to keep the matter quiet, so, in effect, Dionise started to blackmail him. Eventually he escaped by buying her off.

Men might try to escape consequences, but did not always succeed, as Samuel Rowlands wrote in his collection of humorous tales, *Good newes and bad newes*, which were moral warnings based on common occurrences. In one, a young woman comes to London and rises to the position of chambermaid:

58

And therewithal her wages much did mend,
Now like a gentlewoman she doth go,
And country maids admire to see her so,
Telling her friends with all the speed they can,
They will be Londoners like Mistress Anne.

However, in his predictable tale, she is soon made pregnant by 'a scurvy serving-man', who denies responsibility, but in vain:

that same wicked fellow that did this,
Doth vow and swear the child is none of his,
But sets it light, and makes thereof a scoff,
And thinks in knavery to bob her off.
But he'll be talked withal ere one month ends,
For the poor wench hath sent for all her friends,
And then it will be proved plain, at large,
That he's the man must bear the nursing charge.
Since Nan's virginity past help is lost,
They'll teach him what a maidenhead will cost,
What law will do he shall be sure to find,
Because he bears such baseness in his mind.
Meanwhile, be it a daughter or a son,
No remedy, it is so lately done.
Nan's Master and her Mistress both abhor it,
But what says she? *They cannot hang her for it.*

The last line makes for a surprising twist in tone, with the insouciant Nan now provided for. (Simon Forman would have found it all too familiar and probable.) The story does not relate what happened to the child; such seductions, or severely impoverished marriages, produced a number of abandoned babies. Those that survived might be put in orphanages, such as at Christ's Hospital or the Bridewell, where they were often baptised under the name of the place where they were found; thus Mary Porch or Jacob Rakt-out-of-the-Ashes, who was found in a heap of warm ashes.

A more extended account of catching a husband when in need comes from the entertaining satire (perhaps by Thomas Dekker) *The Batchelars Banquet* (1603), which was intended as a humorous warning about married life.

It begins with the story of a young woman who

> hath been wooed, sued, and courted by the bravest gallants
> in that country, of whom one being more forward and
> courageous than the rest, hath offered her such kindness as
> sticks by her ribs a good while after ... by reason of her
> tender compassion and kind acceptance of this proffered
> service, it so falls out she hath played false, as there is no
> other shift but to keep it close, and to take such order as best
> they can for smoothing up of the matter.
>
> [It appears that she cannot marry her seducer] But now
> you must note, that she being but a simple girl between
> fourteen and fifteen years of age, nothing expert ... knows
> not herself how it is with her. But her mother ... having
> somewhat chid her after the common order ... concludes
> thus comfortably: sith it is done, and cannot altogether
> be remedied, she will seek to salve the matter as well as
> she can ... .
>
> Then her mother proceeds thus: 'You know Master
> T. A. that cometh hither so often, he is you see a proper
> young gentleman, and a rich heir. Tomorrow he hath
> appointed to be here again, look that you give him good
> entertainment, and show him good countenance.' The
> mother's instructions being thus given, and the plot laid for
> the fetching in of this kind fool into Lob's pound [trap],
> the next day he cometh in and is on all hands more kindly
> welcomed and entertained. After dinner, having had great
> cheer, the mother falls in talk with the other guests, and this
> frolic novice gets him as near to the daughter as he can, and
> while the others are hard in chat, he takes her by the hand
> and thus begins to court her.
>
> 'Gentlewoman, I would to God you knew my thoughts.'
>
> 'Your thoughts, sir,' quoth she, 'how should I know them
> except you tell them me? It may be you think something you
> are loth to tell.'
>
> 'Not so,' saith he, 'yet I would you knew it without
> telling'.
>
> 'But that,' saith she, 'is unpossible'.

'Then,' quoth he, 'if I might do it without offence, I would adventure to tell you them.'

'Sir,' saith she, 'you may freely speak your pleasure, for I do much assure me of your honesty, that I know you will speak nothing that may procure offence.'

'Then thus,' saith he, 'I acknowledge without feigning, that I am far unworthy of so great favour as to be accepted for your servant, friend and lover, which art so fair, so gentle and every way so gracious, that I may truly say that you are truly replenished with all the good gifts that nature can plant in any mortal creature. But if you would vouchsafe me this undeserved grace, my good will, diligence and continual forwardness to serve and please you should never fail, but I would therein equal the most loyal lover that ever lived, I would esteem you more than anything else, and tender more your good name and credit than mine own.'

'Good sir,' quoth she, 'I heartily thank you for your kind offer, but I pray you speak no more of such matter, for I neither know what love is, nor care for knowing it. This is not the lesson that my mother teacheth me nowadays.'

'Why,' saith he, 'if you please she shall know nothing of it, yet the other day I heard her talk of preferring you in marriage to Master G. R.'

'How say you to that?' quoth she.

'Marry,' thus answers the gentleman, 'if you would vouchsafe to entertain me for your servant, I would never marry, but rely on your favour.'

'But that,' saith she, 'should be no profit to either of us both, and besides it would be to my reproach, which I had not thought you would seek.'

'Nay,' quoth he, 'I had rather die than seek your discredit.'

'Well, sir,' saith she, 'speak no more hereof, for if my mother should perceive it, I were utterly undone.'

And it may be that her mother makes her a sign to give over ... . When it is brought to this pass, the mother makes motion of a journey to be made the next morning, some ten or twelve miles off, to visit or feast with some friend ... . To this motion they all agree, and afterward sit down to supper, where he is placed next to the daughter, who carries herself so toward him with her piercing glances that the young heir is set on fire therewith.

Well, morning comes, they mount on horseback, and by the opinion of them all there is never a horse in the company that can carry double but his, so that he is appointed to have the maiden ride behind him, whereof he is not a little proud, and when he feels her hold him fast by the middle (which she doth to stay herself the better) he is even ravished with joy. After their return home, which will be the same night, the mother, taking her daughter aside, questions with her all that had passed between the amorous gallant and her ... .

The next morning [the daughter] walks into the garden, and this lusty younker follows, when, having given her the time of day, he falls to his former suit. She wills him to give over such talk, or she will leave his company.

'Is this the love you bear me,' quoth she 'to seek my dishonesty? You know well enough that my father and mother is minded to bestow me otherwise.'

'Ah, my sweet mistress,' saith he, 'I would they did so far favour me herein as they do him; I dare boldly say and swear it, and without vainglory utter it, that I am every way his equal.'

'Oh sir,' answers she, 'I would he were like you.'

'Ah, sweet mistress,' saith he, 'you deign to think better of me than I deserve, but if you would further vouchsafe me the other favour, I should esteem myself most happy.'

'In troth, sir,' saith she, 'it is a thing I may not do of myself, without the counsel and consent of my parents, to whom I would gladly move it, if I thought they would not be offended. But it should be better if yourself would break the matter unto them, and be sure, if that they refer the matter to me, you shall speed so soon as any.'

He, being ravished with these words, and yielding her infinite thanks, trots presently to the mother to get her good will. To be short, with a little ado the matter is brought about, even in such sort as he would desire, they are straightway contracted and immediately wedded, both because her friends fear that the least delay will prevent all, and because he is so hot in the spur that he thinks every hour a year till it be done. Well, the wedding night comes, wherein she behaves herself so by her mother's counsel that he dares swear upon the Bible that he had her maidenhead, and that he himself was the first that trod the path.

* * * * *

The Wedding Day

After all the courting and contracting, people could not go off and get married whenever they fancied. Marriage was not approved by the Church at certain times of the year – during Advent and Christmas, during part of Lent and from Rogation Sunday to Trinity Sunday. A rhyme provided a helpful reminder:

> Advent marriage doth thee deny,
> But Hilary gives thee liberty.
> Septuagesima says thee nay,
> Eight days from Easter says you may.
> Rogation bids thee to contain,
> But Trinity sets thee free again.

In medieval times, marriages took place in the church porch (Chaucer's Wife of Bath had been there five times, 'withouten other companye in youthe'), but by Elizabeth's time it was celebrated in the church, with prayers and communion, and exchange of rings. The ceremony included the words, 'With this ring I thee wed … and with my body I thee worship.' The phrasing derived from the Middle Ages, and continued in the Protestant Prayer Book of 1548. In their *Admonition to Parliament* in 1572, Puritans objected to the wording, on the grounds that, having got rid of idolatry of images of saints and the Virgin Mary, the idolatry of the worship of the body should be discontinued – but it was retained (for hundreds of years). People generally dressed up for the occasion, according to their circumstances, though the bride did not usually wear white.

Thomas Deloney's story, *Jacke of Newberie* (1597) provides a picture of a showy wedding (to celebrate the success of the hero, a celebrated clothier):

> So the marriage day being appointed, all things prepared meet for the wedding, and royal cheer ordained, most of the lords, knights and gentlemen thereabout were invited thereunto [it is just a story]; the bride being attired in a gown of sheep's russet and a kirtle of fine worsted, her head attired with a biliment [ornamental band] of gold, and her hair as yellow as gold hanging down behind her, which was curiously combed and plaited according to the manner of those days. She was led to church between two sweet boys, with bride-laces and rosemary tied about their silken sleeves; the one of them was son to Sir Thomas Parry, the other to Sir Francis Hungerford. Then was there a fair bride-cup of silver and gilt carried before her, hung about with silken ribbons of all colours; next was there a noise [band] of musicians, that played all the way before her; after her came all the chiefest maidens of the country, some bearing great bride-cakes and some garlands of wheat finely gilded, and so she passed into the church … .
>
> The marriage being solemnized, home they came in order as before, and to dinner they went, where was no want of good cheer, no lack of melody; Rhenish wine at this wedding was as plentiful as beer or ale, for the merchants had sent thither ten tuns of the best in the Stillyard [storehouse in London]. This wedding endured ten days, to the great relief of the poor that dwelt all about; and in the end the bride's father and mother came to pay their daughter's portion, which when the bridegroom had received, he gave them great thanks.

It's all exaggerated for the purposes of this 'local boy made good' romance, but gives an idea of how a wealthy wedding might be. Celebrations could be protracted and lively, as the presence here of the musicians and quantities of wine and beer might suggest. Even Petruchio, in *The Taming of the Shrew*, promises Katherine jollifications, when they will

revel it as bravely as the best,
With silken coats and caps, and golden rings,
With ruffs and cuffs and farthingales and things,
With scarves and fans and double change of bravery,
With amber bracelets, beads, and all this knavery.

After the wedding would come the ritual of the bedding of the bride: as Edmund Spenser wrote in his *Epithalamion* (wedding poem) of 1594: 'Now bring the Bryde into the bridal bourse, / Now night is come, now soon her disarray.' An account of the wedding of Sir Philip Herbert (a favourite of King James) to the Earl of Oxford's daughter in 1604 records, 'No ceremony was omitted of bride-cakes, points, garters and gloves, which been ever since the livery of the Court; and at night there was sewing into the sheet, casting off the bride's left hose, with many other pretty sorceries.' King James also took part in more of the fun and games than might have been wished.

A Frenchman, Henri Misson, in his *Memoirs and Observations in his Travels over England* (translated 1719), wrote an account of typical gentry or middle-class weddings:

When bedtime is come, the bridesmen pull off the bride's garters, which she had before untied that they might hang down and so prevent a curious hand coming too near her knee. This done, and the garters being fastened to the hats of the gallants, the bridesmaids carry the bride into the bedchamber, where they undress her and lay her in bed. The bridegroom, who by the help of his friends is undressed in some other room, comes in his nightgown as soon as possible to his spouse, who is surrounded by mother, aunts, sisters and friends, and without any further ceremony gets into bed. Some of the women run away, others remain, and the moment afterwards they are all got together again. The bridesmen take the bride's stockings, and the bridesmaids the bridegroom's; both sit down at the bed's feet and fling the stocking over their heads, endeavouring to direct them so as that they may fall upon the married couple. If the man's stocking thrown by the maid fall upon the bridegroom's head, it is a sign she will quickly be married herself; and the same prognostic holds good of the woman's stocking thrown by the man. Oftentimes these young people engage with one another upon the success of the stockings, though they themselves look upon it to be nothing but sport.

While some amuse themselves agreeably with these little follies, others are preparing a good posset, which is a kind of caudle, a potion made up of milk, wine, yolks of eggs, sugar, cinnamon, nutmeg, etc. This they present to the young couple, who swallow it down as fast as they can to get rid of so troublesome company; the bridegroom prays, scolds, entreats them to be gone, and the bride says ne'er a word, but thinks the more. If they obstinately continue to retard the accomplishment of their wishes, the bridegroom jumps up in his shirt, which frightens the women and puts them to flight. The men follow them, and the bridegroom turns to the bride.

Chapter 4

Married Life

There belongeth more to marriage than four bare legs in a bed.
(Elizabethan proverb)

Sir Francis Bacon, philosopher, was ambivalent about the whole business:

> He that hath a wife and children hath given hostages to fortune ... . Certainly, wife and children are a kind of discipline of humanity; and single men, though they be many times more charitable, because their means are less exhausted, yet on the other side, they are more cruel and hard-hearted ... . Wives are young men's mistresses; companions for middle age; and old men's nurses. So a man may have a quarrel to marry when he will. But he was reputed one of the wise men, that made answer to the question, when a man should marry: A young man not yet, an older man not at all.

The Paradise of Married Women

In Elizabethan England, marriage was fundamental to the social structure and to the relationships of the sexes, to their economic relationships and to the balance of power. In an intensely hierarchical and patriarchal society, the husband's authority was axiomatic, in theory, at least, with the wife having few legal rights. For men, marriage established them, ostensibly, as stable, responsible members of their community. Since St Paul, the woman had been described as 'the weaker vessel'. One homily on marriage, ordered to be read in church, declared that:

> The woman is a weak creature not endued with the like strength and constancy of mind; therefore they be the sooner

67

disquieted, and they be the more prone to all weak affections and dispositions of mind, more than men be; and lighter they be, and more vain in their fantasies and opinions.[1]

As such, they needed to be kept in order, by fathers or husbands.

When it came to marriage, the consequences could be more significant for women, setting future patterns of living, work (most lower and middle-class women contributed to the household finances), social life and status. Their very identity depended on their husbands and, in the probable event of remarriage, that identity might be very changeable, according to his status, wealth and character.

In principle, marital order derived from and paralleled social order. The cleric William Whateley, in his *A bride-bush: A directive for married persons* (1619), explained that, 'The man must be taken for God's immediate officer in the house, and as it were the king in the family; the woman must account herself his deputy, an officer substituted to him, not as an equal, but as subordinate.'[2] As the subordinate, she was in effect the husband's property. In *The Taming of the Shrew*, Petruchio, when married, expresses this with characteristic, if shocking, bluntness (while remembering the Tenth Commandment):

> I will be master of what is mine own:
> She is my goods, my chattels, she is my house,
> My household stuff, my field, my barn,
> My horse, my ox, my ass, my any thing.

Not all his auditors at the time would have gone along altogether with this – notably the other women characters in the play – but everyone knew the theory. Sir Thomas Overbury, in his *Characters* (published in 1614), in describing 'A Good Wife' starts from the principle of possession, but more positively:

> A man's best movable, a scion incorporate with the stock, bringing sweet fruit; one that to her husband is more than a friend, less than trouble; an equal with him in the yoke. Calamities and troubles she shares alike, nothing pleases her that doth not him. She is relative in all, and he without

her but half himself. She is his absent hands, eyes, ears and mouth; his present and absent all … a husband without her is a misery.

There were, of course, plenty of contented marriages, but these did not make interesting material for writers. Samuel Rowlands, in *'Tis Merry when Gossips Meet* (1612), cites a shopkeeper tenderly asking his wife, 'What ails my sweetheart, tell me, honey,/ My love, my dove, my lamb, my pretty coney.' Companionate marriages tended not to figure largely in the drama; Shakespeare provides the companionate marriage of Julius Caesar and Calpurnia, and that of the Macbeths, where he calls his wife, 'love' and 'dearest chuck'.

The puritan William Gouge, in his *Domesticall Duties* (1622), goes further into the marital relationship. A husband's 'look, his speech, his carriage and his actions wherein he has to do with his wife must be seasoned with love: love must show itself in his commandments, in his reproofs, in his instructions'; with all this authoritarianism, there is also an equality: 'as betwixt man and wife in the power of one another's bodies: for the wife (as well as in the husband) is therein both a servant and a mistress, a servant to yield her body, a mistress to have the power of his.'[3]

When it came to sexual intercourse, church teaching and the double standard meant that the young woman should have no experience, and the man very little, and not be well informed. Medically, sexuality was understood in terms of the four humours, a theory that looked back to classical Greece. Hippocrates described the four fluids that controlled the body, that is, blood, yellow bile, black bile and phlegm, which needed to be kept in balance; later, Galen developed the theory of the four humours – hot, cold, moist and dry – and linked them with the four temperaments, sanguine, choleric, melancholic and phlegmatic. A man's seed developed within his body as a result of the digestive process: some blood was changed within his testicles to semen. The woman had female testicles to form female semen. Sexual appetite would be stimulated by red meat, sugar and wine; better digestion produced more blood, so giving more to the testicles and stimulating the sexual appetite. A ballad from around 1590 told the tale of a young woman 'afraid to die a maid', until a man 'gave her well of Watkins Ale', with predictable results nine months later.

The best-known sex manual, *Aristotle's Masterpiece, or the Secrets of Generation* (1684), was of no practical assistance, merely providing some unreliable physical facts. In general, authorities recommended restricted sexual activity in marriage: abstinence in summer, during menstruation and the later stages of pregnancy. Those with a theological background were particularly unhelpful: 'Nothing is more impure than to love a wife like an adulterous woman.' On the other hand, the Church emphasised that sex should be for procreation and, as it was believed that conception required the woman's orgasm, so couples should try to encourage this. Edmund Tilney, in *The Flower of Friendship* (1565), urged the husband to bring this about: 'The wise man may not be contented with his spouse's virginity [inexperience and inhibition], but little and little must presently procure that he may also steal away her private will and appetite, so that two bodies there may be made one only heart.'[4] It has also been argued that 'the very late marriage pattern of north-west Europe, coupled with the low illegitimacy rate, meant that both parties at the time of marriage must have had some ten years' experience of masturbation, and that this habit was likely to inhibit satisfactory sexual relations in marriage.'[5] In the first few of Shakespeare's *Sonnets*, he implicitly accuses a young man, apparently loath to marry, of masturbatory narcissism: 'Unthrifty loveliness, why dost thou spend / Upon thyself thy beauty's legacy? … . For having traffic with thyself alone, / Thou of thyself thy sweet self dost deceive': he has been wasting what could have gone to implanting a child.

As it was, marital sexual activity among the [rural] poor apparently varied from month to month according to the demands of agricultural work, as indicated by church birth registers. There appears to have been a decline in conceptions in March, August and September, with a peak in early spring and later in autumn. With relatively late marriages – mid-twenties for most women – and the menopause tending to begin earlier than in modern times, there were not very many child-bearing years available. William Harrison, uncomprehending of the effects of the menopause, wrote how 'our women through bearing of children do after forty begin to wrinkle apace.'

London in particular was unhealthy, with frequent visitations of the plague every four years or so, when several thousand might die. It is no wonder that Thomas Nashe wrote in his famous song, *Adieu, farewell earth's bliss* (1592), the verse:

70

Rich men, trust not in wealth,
　Gold cannot buy you health,
Physic himself must fade;
　All things to end are made;
The plague full swift goes by;
I am sick, I must die;
　Lord have mercy on us …

Then, of course, there was smallpox; malaria from the marshy ground south of the river, which was excellent breeding grounds for mosquitoes; infections from the open drains and dung-carts; agues, and 'tertian' and 'quartan' fevers. People also complained of the smoke (coals from Newcastle and Kent). Inevitably, there were high mortality rates for adults as well as children. Shakespeare, though he retired from London, died at 52, which was about the average for theatre people (of his seven siblings, only one got past 42); upper-class men averaged in the low sixties. Marriages might not last very long and infant mortality rates were high: about one quarter of children died before the age of 10 (Hamnet Shakespeare died in 1596, aged 11). Families in moderately well-off Cheapside, near the successful market, averaged about four surviving children, but those in poorer Clerkenwell only averaged two and a half. It depended on where one lived. Perhaps Nashe was not quite right: then as now, wealth could buy health.

London needed a constant inflow of young country people for service and apprenticeships – the inflow doubled in the second half of the century. The poor produced fewer children than the upper classes (perhaps one per cent of women died in childbirth and matters were worse in the poorer parts of London), whose women tended not to breastfeed their babies but put them out to wet nurses (as lactation discouraged menstruation). Anne Donne, wife of John Donne, courtier and MP, who married without parental consent at 17, had eleven pregnancies in fourteen years, dying after the second stillbirth.

Putting babies out to nurse, or sending young children to foster parents, might diminish close affection between parents and children, with the latter often in warmer relationships with servants. In his *Civile Conversation*, Stephen Guazzo writes of a child saying bitterly to its mother, 'You bore me but nine months in your belly, but my nurse kept me with her teats the space of two years … . So soon as I was born,

71

you deprived me of your company, and banished me your presence.'[6] Other texts show much more positive pictures of motherly love, as in a book intended for French readers, Peter Erondell's *The French Garden* (1605). All the phrases that the woman might need are included, which makes the mother seem unusually effusive, but a good sense of domestic life is suggested. Here, a well-to-do lady visits her baby, and tells the nurse:

> Unswaddle him, undo his swaddling bands, give him his breakfast while I am here, make his pap … . Wash him before me, have you clean water? O my little heart! God bless thee. Rub the crown of his head, with his ears … wash his face: lift up a little his hairs, is not that some dust I see upon his forehead? … His little cheeks are wet, I believe you did let him alone to cry and weep; pick his nostrils, wipe his mouth and his lips. How many teeth has he? … Pull off his shirt, thou art pretty and fat my little darling … . His thumb and little finger are flea-bitten, for the black spots are there yet, is there any fleas in your chamber? … Now swaddle him again, but first put on his biggin [cap] and his little band [soft collar] with an edge, where is his little petticoat? Give him his coat of changeable taffeta, and his satin sleeves. Where is his bib? Let him have his gathered apron with strings, and hang a muckinder [bib] to it. You need not yet to give him his coral with the small golden chain [a teething ring] … . Give him some suck, I pray you take heed to wipe well the nipple of your dug before you put it in his mouth, for fear that there be any hair or other thing that may hurt him. You, maid, go fetch the child's cradle, make his bed, where is his pillow? … Put him in his cradle and rock him till he sleep, but bring him to me first that I may kiss him. God send thee good rest, my little boykin. I pray you, good nurse, have a care of him.

And after this, she goes away.

There was little available by way of 'family planning'. Various herbs were thought to be effective contraceptives: rue, for example, or savin, (an oil traditionally used to bring on menstruation, nicknamed 'cover-shame', and described as 'a notorious restorative of slender shapes and tender reputations', presumably with the unmarried in mind[7]). Otherwise, traditional unsatisfying techniques, such as coitus interruptus, were used. Anal intercourse was by no means unknown; Simon Forman thought Emilia Lanier practised it. In Marston's *The Insatiate Countess* (1606), two wives discuss thwarting some proposed wife-swapping by exchanging bedrooms at night. When one asks, 'You mean they shall come in at the back door?', the other insists, 'Who, our husbands? Nay, and they come not in at the fore-door, there will be no pleasure in't.'

Those who liked to tell people how to behave wrote that wives should be, first of all, housewives. Thus Robert Dod and John Cleaver, in *A godly form of household government* (1598), describe the virtuous wife: 'Let her avoid such occasions as may draw her from her calling. She must shake off sloth and love of ease. She must avoid gossiping further than the law of good neighbourhood doth require. St Paul would have a woman a good *homekeeper.*'

The authors' insistence on 'must' suggests a losing battle. Foreigners saw matters somewhat differently, and thought English wives had relatively good lives. The Dutchman, Emanuel Van Meteren, wrote of comfortably-off wives, and how

> They are not kept so strictly as they are in Spain or elsewhere. Nor are they shut up, but they have the free management of the house or housekeeping, after the fashion of the Netherlands and others their neighbours. They go to market to buy what they like best to eat. They are well dressed, fond of taking it easy, and commonly leave the care of household matters and drudgery to their servants. They sit before their doors, decked out in fine clothes, in order to see and be seen by the passers-by ... . All the rest of their time they employ in walking or riding, or playing cards or otherwise, or visiting their friends and keeping company, conversing with their equals (whom they term gossips) and their neighbours, and making merry with them at childbirths, christenings, churchings and funerals; and all this with the permission and knowledge of their husbands, as such is the

custom ... . This is why England is called the paradise of married women.

Another foreigner, Thomas Platter, remarked on married women visiting taverns in hen parties, where the

> women as well as the men, in fact more than they, will frequent the taverns or alehouses for enjoyment. They count it a great honour to be taken there and given wine with sugar to drink; and if one woman is invited, she will bring three or four other women along and they gaily toast each other; the husband afterwards thanks him who has given his wife such pleasure, for they deem it a real kindness.

The idea of paradisal England was still prevalent a century later, when in 1678 John Ray took up the phrase

> England is the paradise of women. And well it may be called so, as might easily be demonstrated in many particulars, were not all the world already therein satisfied. Hence it hath been said, that if a bridge were made over the narrow seas all the women in Europe would come over hither. Yet it is worth noting that though in no country of the world the men are so fond of, so much governed by, so much wedded to their wives, yet hath no language so many proverbial invectives against women.[8]

* * * * *

Gallantly Attired

As it was, some features that Van Meteren commended were criticised, such as the habit of women sitting before their doors, dressed up or merely chatting with neighbours. There were references to such texts as Proverbs IX.14-18, where a woman 'sitteth at the door of her house ... . To call passengers who go right on their ways ... . Whoso is simple, let him turn in thither ... her guests are in the depths of hell.'

Women's dressing up and fashions were condemned, as they suggested immorality, vanity and social disorder (dressing above one's social status). Women, puritans or jealous, as well as men might join in such attacks. One husband, William Vaughan, even wrote a treatise in response to defamatory rumours about his wife's dressing up, how some people

> do but gather by presumptions and circumstances, that chaste women prostitute their bodies because they go gallantly attired in the fashion, with strange periwigs, with false bodies, trunk sleeves, verdingales, and with costly jewels, belike beyond their husbands' means ... because they go to stage plays, to public dances and shows upon Sundays and Holy-days.[9]

Among the fashions most criticised or derided was for false hair and elaborate hairstyles. The Elizabethan dramatist John Lyly mocked this in his *Midas* (c. 1584), where a maid and a manservant converse:

> Maid: 'My mistress would rise, and lacks your worship to fetch her hair.'
>
> Manservant: 'Why, is it not on her head?'
>
> Maid: 'No. Methinks it would be, but I mean the hair she must wear today.'
>
> Manservant: 'Why, doth she wear any but her own?'
>
> Maid: 'In faith, sir, I am sure it is her own when she pays for it.'

Later, Licio comments on Celia's hair: 'The purtenances ... it is impossible to reckon them up, much less to tell the nature of them. Hoods, frontlets, wires, cauls, curling-irons, periwigs, bodkins, fillets, hairlaces, ribbons, rolls, knotstrings, glasses, combs, caps, hats, coifs, kerchers, clothes, ear-rings, borders, crippins [curlers], shadows, spots, and so many other trifles.' The servant suggests, 'I note one thing ... that if every part require as much as the head, it will make the richest husband in the world ache at the heart.'

Cosmetic aids were used and, of course, condemned. In Ben Jonson's misogynistic comedy, *Epicoene* (1609), Clerimont sings:

> Still to be neat, still to be dressed,
> As you were going to a feast,
> Still to be powdered, still perfumed,
> Lady, it is to be presumed,
> Though art's hid causes are not found,
> All is not sweet, all is not sound.

The innuendo is that cosmetics cover disease. On the other hand, not all men objected, and some enjoyed women's display. So Jonson's Truewit declares, 'I love a good dressing before any beauty in the world … . If she have good ears, show 'em; good hair, lay it out; good legs, wear short clothes.' In Marston's *The Malcontent* (1604), the Court bawd offers two ladies a potion:

> This it doth, it purefieth the blood, smootheth the skin, enliveneth the eye, strengtheneth the veins, mundefieth the teeth, comforteth the stomach, fortifieth the back, and quickeneth the wit, that's all … . Eat me of this posset, quicken your blood, and preserve your beauty. Do you know Doctor Plaster-face? By this curd, he is the most exquisite in forging of veins, sprightening of eyes, dyeing of hair, sleeking of skins, blushing of cheeks, surfling [whitening] of breasts, blanching and bleaching of teeth, that ever made an old lady gracious by torchlight, by this curd, la! … . Men say! Let them say what they will: life o' women! They are ignorant of your wants.

The cosmetics that were available were not always good to use. In 1598, Richard Haydocke translated from the Italian *A Tracte Containing the Artes of Curious Paintinge*, noting that

> Some women use Sublimate [of mercury] diversely prepared for increase of their beauty. Some bray [pound] it with quicksilver … others boil it in water and therewith wash their face … . But this is sure, that which way soever it be used, it is very offensive to man's flesh … . Wherefore

such women as use it about their face have always black teeth standing far out of their gums like a Spanish mule, an offensive breath, with a face half scorched, and an unclean complexion ... . So that simple women, thinking to grow more beautiful, become disfigured, hastening old age before the time, and giving occasion to their husbands to seek strangers instead of their wives, with divers other inconveniences.

Court ladies' fashions came in for particular condemnation, as from Thomas Nashe in *Christ's Tears over Jerusalem* (1593):

Their heads, with their top and top-gallant [ships' upper sails] lawn baby-caps and snow-resembling silver curtains, they make a plain puppet-stage of. Their breasts they embusk up on high, and their round roseate buds immodestly lay forth, to show at their hands there is fruit to be hoped ... they show the swellings of their minds in the swellings and plumping-out of their apparel ... . Gorgeous ladies of the Court, it is not your pinches [pleats], your purls [frills], your flowery jaggings [cut fringes], but the puffings up of your souls which therein you express.

He also attacked the pursuit of fashion at lower social levels, in *The Seaven Deadly Sinnes of London* (1606) (there is always a market for reactionary grumbling about women):

For as man is God's ape, striving to make artificial flowers, birds, &c like to the natural: so for the same reason are women *Men's She Apes*, for they will not be behind them the breadth of a tailor's yard (which is nothing to speak of) [yard was a euphemism for penis] in any new-fangled upstart fashion. If men get up French-standing collars, women will have the French standing collar too; if doublets with little thick skirts (so short that none are able to sit upon them), women's foreparts are thick-skirted too; by surfeiting upon which kind of fantastical apishness in a short time, they fall into the disease of Pride.

In Thomas Heywood's play, *If you know not me you know nobody* (1602), a London tailor and a pedlar discuss country women's fashions. Says pedlar Tawney, reporting on his trade:

> Faith, sir, our country girls are akin to your London courtiers: every month sick of a new fashion. The horning busk and silken bride-laces are in good request with the parson's wife; your huge poking-stick, and French periwig, with chambermaids and waiting-gentlewomen. Now, your Puritan's poker is not so huge, but somewhat longer; a long slender poking-stick is the all in all with your Suffolk Puritan. [Poking-sticks were stiffeners for large ruffs; the sexual innuendo here is obvious.] Your silk band, half-farthingales, and changeable foreparts are common; not a wench of thirteen but wears a changeable forepart.

> Tailor Hobson: 'An ancient wearing; there's some changeable stuff has been a wear with women time out of mind.' [Foreparts were like stomachers; but the suggestion here is of a covering of pregnancy.]

> Tawney: 'Besides, sir, many of our young married men have taken order to wear yellow garters, points, and shoe-tyings; and 'tis thought yellow will grow a custom.' [In the same year, Malvolio in *Twelfth Night* is to look foolish in yellow stockings.]

> Hobson: ''Tis been used long in London.'

> Tawney: 'And 'tis thought 'twill come in request in the country, too; for a fashion that three or four young wenches have promised me their husbands shall wear, or they miss of their marks. Then your mask, silk-laced, washed gloves, carnation [flesh-coloured] girdles, and busk-paint suitable, as common as coals from Newcastle; you shall not have a kitchen-maid scrape trenchers without her washed gloves, a dairy-maid will not ride to market to sell her butter-milk without her mask and her busk.'

Hobson: 'Still a good hearing. Let the country pay well for their pride; 'tis gratis here in London.'

Apart from the copying of men's fashions that Nashe criticised, women's adaptation, or even wearing, of men's clothing was particularly condemned, even feared, as socially and sexually revolutionary. In his *Anatomy of Abuses* (1583), Philip Stubbes complains of the taking of

> attire appropriate only to men, yet they blush not to wear it, and if they could as well change their sex ... I think they would as verily become men indeed as now they degenerate from godly, sober women ... . Our apparel was given as a sign distinctive to discern between sex and sex, and therefore one to wear the apparel of the other sex is to participate with the same, and to adulterate the verity of his own kind. Wherefore these women may not improperly be called *hermaphroditi*, that is monsters of both kinds, half women, half men ... not natural women but artificial women, not women of flesh and blood, but rather puppets or mammets of rags and clouts compact together. So far hath this canker of pride eaten into the body of the commonwealth that every poor yeoman his daughter, every husbandman his daughter, and every cottager his daughter will not spare to flaunt it out, in such gowns, petticoats and kirtles as these.

In 1598, William Goddard asked, rhetorically:

> To see Morilla in her coach to ride,
> With her long lock of hair upon one side,
> With hat and feather worn i'th'swaggering'st guise,
> With buttoned bodice skirted doublet-wise,
> Unmasked and sit i'th'boot without a fan,
> Speak: could you judge her less than some man?
> If less. Then I'm sure you'd judge at least,
> She was part man, part woman; part a beast.[10]

In the early 1600s, the pamphlets *Hic-Mulier* and *Haec-Vir*, attacking fashionable gender ambiguity, criticised women's wearing of male clothing, abandoning 'the comely hood, caul, coif, handsome dress or kerchiefs' for 'the cloudy ruffianly broad-brimmed hat and wanton feather … the loose lascivious embracement of a French doublet, being all unbuttoned to entice … shorn, powdered, borrowed hair, a naked, lascivious, bawdy bosom.'

Exposing the breasts was a fashion, frequently condemned, that developed in the second half of the century, making its way up from the lower reaches of society to young ladies, especially the unmarried. In a 'moral interlude' (play) of 1566, *The life and Repentance of Marie Magdalene,* by Lewis Wager, a young woman is instructed by the Vices how to seduce:

> Your garments must be worn always
> That your white paps may be seen, if you may.
> If young gentlemen may see your white skin
> It will allure them to love, and soon bring 'em in.
> Both damsels and wives use many feats,
> I know them here that will lay out their fair teats,
> Purposely men to allure unto their love.

In his *Court of Vertue* (1565), John Hall (born 1529) wrote:

> When I was a boy, I now well remember
> (Though I at that time of age were but tender)
> That women their breasts did show and lay out,
> And well was that maid whose dugs were stout.
> Which usance at first came up in the stews,
> Which men's wives and daughters after did use.

Apart from exposing their breasts, some women wore men's clothing with aggressive provocation. In 1585, the Essex Church court heard how 'Hunt's wife, contrary to God's law, did put on men's apparel and went forth from one house to another so ungodly and shamefully, with other naughtiness of words', and in 1592 it heard how the wife of Jacob Cornell 'useth to wear young men's garters and said she would do so till they came for them.'[11]

* * * * *

No Slender Maintenance

Thomas Dekker's warning to young men not to marry, *The Batchelors Banquet*, included lively comedy about married life. Regarding wives wanting to dress up, he writes how the wife

> must be maintained according to her degree, and withal (commonly it happens [if] she carry the right stomach of a woman) slender maintenance will not serve, for as their minds mount above their estates, so commonly will they have their habiliments [dress]. And if at a feast or some other gossips' meeting whereunto she is invited, she see any of the company gaily attired for cost, or fashion, or both, and chiefly the latter (for generally women affect novelties) she forthwith moves a question to herself why she also should not be in like sort attired … . Awaiting only fit time and place for the moving of her husband thereto … observing her opportunity when she might take her husband at most advantage, which is commonly in the bed, the garden of love, the state of marriage delights, and the life wherein the weaker sex hath ever the better: when therefore this lusty gallant would prosecute his desired pleasures, for which cause he chiefly ran wilfully into the peril of Lob's pound, then squeamishly she begins thus, saying, 'I pray you husband let me alone, trouble me not, for I am not well at ease.' Which he hearing, presently makes this reply, 'Why, my sweetheart, what ails you, are you not well? I pray thee, wife, tell me, where lies thy grief?'
>
> [Eventually she is persuaded to reply.] 'Well, husband, if you will needs, you shall. You know on Thursday last, I was sent for, and you willed me, to go to Mistress M.'s churching, and when I came thither I found great cheer, and no small company of wives; but the meanest of them all was not so ill attired as I, and surely I was never so ashamed of myself in my life, yet I speak it not to praise myself. But it is well known, and I dare boldly say, that the best woman there came of no better stock than I. But, alas, I speak not this for myself, for God wot I pass not how meanly I am apparelled, but I speak it for your credit and my friends.'

'Why, wife,' saith he, 'of what calling and degree were those you speak of?'

'Truly, good husband,' saith she, 'the meanest that was there, being but of my degree, was in her gown with trunk sleeves, her farthingale, her turkey grosgrain kirtle, her taffety hat with a gold band, and these with the rest of her attire made of the newest fashion, which is known the best. Whereas I, poor wretch, had on my threadbare gown, which was made me so long ago, against I was married ... since which time I am grown very much, and so charged with cares and griefs, that I look far older than I am.' [The husband has various financial difficulties, but after several quarrels, gives in.] His wife, now being sure of all, begins to curse the first inventors of pride, and excess in apparel, saying, 'Fie upon it, what pride is this? But I pray you, husband, do not say hereafter that I made you lay out your money in this needless sort, for I protest that I have no delight or desire to go thus garishly. If I have [enough] to cover my body and keep me warm it contents me.' Whereas before she vaunted that she could find in her heart to keep always within doors, she will be sure now every good day to go abroad, and at each feast and gossips' meeting to be a continual guest, that all may see her bravery, and how well she doth become it; to which cause she also comes every Sunday daily to church, that there she may see and be seen, which her husband thinks she doth of mere devotion.

Dekker then goes on to deal with activities associated with childbearing – pregnancy and lying-in:

There is another humour incident to a woman, when her husband sees her belly to grow big (though peradventure by the help of some other friend, yet he persuades himself it is a work of his own framing); and this breeds in him new cares and troubles, for then must he trot up and down day and night, far and near, to get with great cost that his wife longs for. If she lets fall but a pin, he is diligent to take it up, lest she by stooping should hurt herself.

But when the time draws near of her lying down, then must he trudge to bid gossips, such as she will appoint, or else all the fat is in the fire. Consider then what cost and trouble it will be to him to have all things fine against the christening day, what store of sugar, biscuits, comfits and carraways, marmalade and marzipan, with all kinds of sweet suckets and superfluous banqueting stuff … . Besides the charge of the midwife, she must have her nurse to attend and keep her, who must make for her warm broths, and costly caudles, enough both for herself and for her mistress, being of the mind to fare no worse than she.

As to the birth itself, Dekker admits:

I deny not that when a woman is with child, she bides many times great pains, and is oft very ill at ease, and at the time of her deliverance she is for the most part not only in exceeding pain, but also in no less danger of death. But all this is nothing to the husband's troubles, on whose hands alone rests the whole charge and weight of maintaining the house and dispatching all matters … .

Then every day after her lying-down, will sundry dames visit her, which are her neighbours, her kinswomen and other her special acquaintances, whom the good man must welcome with all cheerfulness, and be sure there be some dainties in store to set before them, where they about some three or four hours (or possible half a day) will sit chatting with the childwife, and by that time the cups of wine have merrily trolled about, and half a dozen times moistened their lips with the sweet juice of the purple grapes, they begin thus to discourse.

'Good Lord, neighbour, I marvel how our gossip Free doth, I have not seen the good soul this many a day.'

'Ah, God help her,' quoth another, 'for she hath her hands full of work, and her heart full of heaviness. While she drudges all the week at home, her husband like an unthrift never leaves running abroad, to the tennis court and dicing houses, spending all that ever he hath in such lewd sort. Yea, and if that were worst it were well. But hear ye, gossip, there is another matter spoils all, he cares no more for his wife than for a dog, but keeps queans [whores] even under her nose.'

'Jesu,' saith another, 'who would think he were such a man, he behaves himself so orderly and civil, to all men's sights.'

'Tush, hold your peace, gossip,' saith the other, 'It is commonly seen, the still sow eats up all the draff. He carries a smooth countenance, but a corrupt conscience. That I know F well enough, I will not say he loves Mistress G. Go to, gossip, I drink to you.'

'Yea,' saith another, 'there goes foul lies if G himself loves not his maid N. I can tell their mouths will not be stopped with a bushel of wheat that speak it.'

Then the third, fetching a great sigh, saying, 'by my troth, such another bold bettress [betrayer] have I at home. For never give me credit, gossip, if I took her not the other day in close confidence with her master, but I think I beswaddled [beat] my maid in such sort, that she will have small list to do so again.'

'Nay, gossip,' saith another, 'had it been to me, that should not have served her turn, but I would have turned the quean out of doors to pick a salad. For, wot ye what, gossip, it is ill setting fire and flax together. But I pray you tell me one thing: when saw you our friend Mistress C? Now, in good sooth, she is a kind creature, and a very gentle peat [little pet]. I promise you I saw her not since you and I drank a pint of wine with her in the fish market.'

'Oh gossip,' saith the other, 'there is great change since that time, for they have been fain to pawn everything they have, and yet, God knows, her husband lies still in prison.'

'O the passion of my heart,' saith another, 'is all their great and glorious show come to nothing? Good Lord, what a world is this.'

'Why, gossip,' saith another, 'it was never like to be otherwise, for they loved ever to go fine, and fare daintily, and, by my fay, gossip, this is not a world for those matters, and thereupon I drink to you.'

This is commonly their communication, where they find cheer according to their class.

* * * * *

Careless Domineering

Whilst some men criticised women for exploiting marriage, women also bewailed the imbalance of the sexes and the dissatisfactions of marriage. In Marston's *The Dutch Courtesan* (1605), his character, the outspoken Crispinella, complains about having to submit to kissing by strangers, a practice particularly enjoyed by foreign visitors:

> By the faith and trust I bear to my face, 'tis grown one of the most unsavoury ceremonies. Body'a beauty, 'tis one of the most unpleasing injurious customs to ladies: any fellow that has but one nose on his face, and standing colour and skirts also lined with taffety sarsenet, must salute us on the lips as familiarly. Soft skins save us, there was a stub-bearded John-a-stile with a ployden's [ploughman's] face saluted me last day, and stroke his bristles through my lips; I ha' spent 10 shillings in pomatum since to skin them again. Marry, if a nobleman or a knight with one look visit us, though his unclean goose-turd green teeth ha' the palsy, his nostrils smell worse than a putrefied marrow-bone, and his loose beard drops into our bosom, yet we must kiss him with a curtsey – a curse – for my part I would as lief they would break wind in my lips.

Crispinella has plenty to say against men and marriage:

> Marry? No, faith, husbands are like lots in the lottery: you may draw forty blanks before you find one that has any price in him. A husband generally is a careless domineering thing that grows like coral, which as long as it is under water is soft and tender, but as soon as it has got his branch above

85

the waves is presently hard stiff, not to be bowed or burst: so when your husband is a suitor and under your choice, Lord, how supple he is, how obsequious, how at your service, sweet lady; once married, got up his head above, a stiff crooked knobby inflexible tyrannous creature hr grows. Then they turn like water: more you would embrace, the less you hold. I'll live my own woman, and if the worst come to the worst, I had rather prove a wag than a fool.

Beatrice: 'O, but a virtuous marriage?'

Crispinella: 'Virtuous marriage? There is no more affinity betwixt virtue and marriage, than between a man and his horse: indeed, virtue gets up upon marriage sometimes, and manageth it in the right way, but marriage is of another piece … . Oh, i'faith, 'tis a fair thing to be married, and a necessary. To hear this word, "must"! If our husbands be proud we must bear his contempt; if noisome [smelly], we must bear with the goat under his armholes, and, which is worse, if a loose liver we must live upon his unwholesome reversions. Where, on the contrary, our husbands, because they can and we must, care not for us. Things hoped with fear and got with strugglings are men's high pleasures, when duty pales and flats their appetites.'

Wandering husbands, 'loose livers', could provide 'unwholesome reversions', as a 1609 ballad, *A Marry'd Woman's Case*, pointed out:

> A woman that's to a whoremonger wed
> Is in a most desperate case.
> She scarce dares to perform her duty in bed
> With one of condition so base:
> For sometimes he's bitten with Turnbull-street fleas –
> The pox or some other infectious disease,
> And yet, to her peril, his lust she must please,
>   Oh! Thus lives a woman that's married.[12]

Conversely, as Crispinella (in Marston's words) inveighed against the husbands' dominance and rule, other writers complained of bossy wives.

Dekker observes in a wife 'an extreme desire of sovereignty (which is known a common fault among women) and to be her husband's commander.' The hen-pecked husband is a frequent character; he appears in a Roxburghe ballad, *My wife will be my Master*:

> I wash the dishes, sweep the house, I dress the wholesome diet;
> I humour her in everything, because I would be quiet;
> Of every several dish of meat, she'll surely be first taster,
> And I am glad to pick the bones, *she is so much my Master* ...
>
> And when I am with her in bed, she doth not use me well, Sir,
> She'll wring my nose, and pull my ears, a pitiful tale to tell, Sir.
> And when I am with her in bed, not meaning to molest her,
> She'll kick me out at her bed's feet, *and so become my Master.*

A frequent complaint from a wife was the husband's drinking, as in this ditty from Samuel Rowlands:[13]

> Thou sittest at the alehouse here,
> While I at home do spare,
> Not caring so thy guts be full,
> How thy poor wife doth fare.
> Thy servants do even what they list,
> Thy children they may starve.
> Hanging's too good for such a rogue,
> Far worse thou dost deserve ...

Wives were encouraged to help their husbands to a more sober life, tactfully. John Taylor, however, gives an example of a shrewish tirade:

> In troth, husband, I can hold no longer, but I must speak;
> I see you will still follow this vein of ill husbandry, never
> keep at home ... . I'faith, this course of life must be
> left ... . Let them look to your shop that will, for I will
> not: keep your shop, and then it will keep you ... you
> began the week well, for this day and no longer, so soon
> as you were up, and ready, then to the alehouse with your
> companions.

By contrast, a 1617 ballad from *'Tis not otherwise* or *The praise of a married life*, has the new husband celebrating the change from rowdy bachelorhood:

> No constable nor watch scare I,
> That crieth, 'Who goes there?'
> Do not reel, but soberly,
> Can pass them void of care:
> I use no caudle in the morn,
> I drink not out mine eyes,
> My wife hath made me these to scorn.

In another ballad from 1629, *The Lamentation of a new married man*, a newly-wed husband regrets his bachelor days and resists his wife's corrections:

> A wife hath won you credit,
> A wife makes you esteemed,
> An honest man through marriage
> Now you are surely deemed.[14]

Men, like women, could be reconciled to the social benefits of marriage. In Samuel Rowlands's *The Bride* (1617), a verse debate between various women, on marriage they agree that, 'were not marriage, we must all believe, / The generations of the earth would cease', so that, in general, marriage is a good thing, and 'a remedy for sin'; they conclude that only

> When every crow shall turn to be a parrot,
> And every star out-shine the glorious sun,
> And the new water-works run white and claret,
> That come to town by way of Islington,
> Women and men shall quite renounce each other,
> And maids shall be with child, like Merlin's mother.

Until then, it is safe for the young bride to marry, for men and women will always want each other.

* * * * *

The perfect image of the ideal Elizabethan lover. (© *Bridgeman Images*)

A young Elizabethan maidservant, possibly hoping for love. (© *Lebrecht History / Bridgeman Images*)

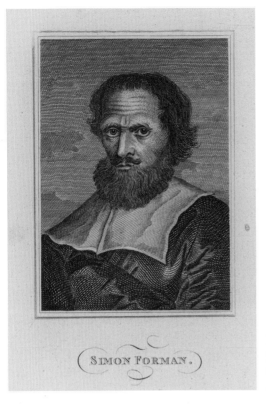

Simon Forman, successful London physician and womaniser.
(© *Look and Learn / Bridgeman Images*)

Mary Frith, a famous, or notorious, cross-dressing performer.
(© *Granger / Bridgeman Images*)

HÆC Exerate

HÆC-VIR:
Or
The Womanish-Man:

She John

Being an Anſwere to a late Booke intituled
Hic-Mulier.

Expreſt in a briefe Dialogue betweene *Hæc-Vir* the Womaniſh-Man, and *Hic-Mulier* the Man-Woman.

Haec-Vir. An image from a pamphlet suggesting unease about women's masculine fashion. (© *British Library Board. All Rights Reserved / Bridgeman Images*)

A middle-class betrothed couple. Her exposed breasts indicate her unmarried status. It appears that their houses are also to be united. (© *Magdalene College, Cambridge [Pepys Library]*)

The wedding night. The newly-weds are put in their four-poster bed by encouraging friends and relatives. (© *Magdalene College, Cambridge [Pepys Library]*)

Above left: Sir Philip Sidney, courtier and celebrated poet. (© *De Agostini Picture Library / Bridgeman Images*)

Above right: Lady Mary Herbert, poet and sister of Sir Philip Sidney. (© *Bridgeman Images*)

Left: Lady Penelope Rich, the model for Philip's fictional Stella. (© *Bridgeman Images*)

Above left: Robert Dudley, Earl of Leicester, soldier, courtier and long-term favourite of the Queen. (© *Universal History Archive/UIG / Bridgeman Images*)

Above right: Robert Devereux, Earl of Essex, soldier and briefly a royal favourite. (© *De Agostini Picture Library / Bridgeman Images*)

Right: Lady Arbella Stuart, unhappy relative of the Queen. (© *Bridgeman Images*)

A 'Sieve Portrait' of the Queen. The sieve was a symbol of virginity. In the background, courtiers parade and strut. (© *Bridgeman Images*)

This World's Paradise

In a patriarchal state ruled over by a woman, there was inevitably unease about the apparent subversion of the traditional, and apparently Biblically authorised, hierarchy of male superiority, set against a loosening of general assumptions about behaviour, and developing social and political disturbance. Partly provoked by these, reactionary misogynistic publications appeared early in the seventeenth century, notably Joseph Swetnam's *The Arraignment of lewde, idle, forward and unconstant women* (1615), answered in turn by tracts in defence of women. Rachel Speght, in her *A Mouzell for Melastomus* (1617) (hardly a catch-penny title) reminded readers '"A virtuous woman," saith Solomon, "is the crown of her husband" (Proverbs 12.14), by which metaphor he showeth both the excellency of such a wife, and what account her husband is to make of her.' Her own aphorism will do well to conclude this section on a positive note: 'Marriage is a merri-age, and this world's Paradise, where there is mutual love.'[15]

Chapter 5

Outside Marriage

The Bawdy Courts

In those days, the Church courts (often referred to as 'the bawdy courts'), driven by a combination of canon law and popular opinion, were kept busy attempting to bring order to the sex lives of ordinary people. Adultery, promiscuity and slanderous accusations of sexual irregularity were their main concern. The surviving records for the county of Essex at this time show a remarkable number of prosecutions for sex offences. Charges came from a variety of sources, including church officials and agitated neighbours. In his *Homilies against Whoredom* (1560), Thomas Becon stressed that it was the duty of Christians to expose and guard against the sexual irregularities of others in the community; accordingly, some people were energetic to denounce the pleasurable improprieties of others. In the fifty-five years between 1548 and 1603, of a population of about 40,000 adults, about 15,000 – perhaps 270 a year – were summonsed for sex offences, ranging from adultery and promiscuity to incest and even rape (though that was a criminal offence, and not for the Church courts):

> In an adult life span of 30 years, an Elizabethan inhabitant of Essex had more than a one-in-four chance of being accused of fornication, adultery, buggery, incest, bestiality or bigamy. Even if only half the charges were well founded, it still suggests a society which was both sexually very lax and also highly inquisitorial, with a great readiness to denounce each other's transgressions.[1]

There were quite a few cases of employers sexually exploiting servants, but punishments might not always follow as one might expect. In one slightly unusual case, Jane Wright bore a child by John Lawrence, a church elder of the parish (so the Church court might have had some prejudice). She claimed that he desired her of a certain night to hold his aching back which she

> refusing was eftsoons required by her dame Joan Lawrence so to do, whereupon she, lying upon the bed in her clothes holding his back a good time until she was a-cold, was desired and enticed by him and his wife that night as at other times to come in naked bed with them two, at what time he had carnal knowledge from time to time, her said dame lying in bed with him and warranting her that she should have no harm, and that the other maids had used to do the like before.

For this, Jane was sentenced to stand in the church porch on a Sunday morning, dressed in a sheet, and confess her fault after the sermon.[2]

Elsewhere, in Worcestershire, there was the sad story of Anne Hunthatche, servant of Roger Beckley, the miller, who on 23 July 1599:

> had a daughter baptized, whose father she confessed to the women before her delivery [when a woman was to be delivered of a bastard, the local women would interrogate her during her delivery to name the father, so as to spare the parish the expense of looking after the child], with great protestations, taking the name of God to witness, to be one John Heekes, late servant of John Goffe of Pepleton; but the fame was that the said Roger Beckley was, and is, the father of the said child (but God knoweth). And on Friday the 27th of July, the said mother to the said child was found drowned in the brook adjoining to the mill there. And upon the 28th day of July. Thomas Savage, gent., one of the coroners of her majesty's for the county, empanelled a jury according to order, and by the said jury, she, the said Anne, was found guilty of her own death, and buried in the highway on the heath, having an heap of stones laid over her, and a stake driven through her corpse, as the law requireth.[3]

Remarkable and unusual carryings-on might take place in some other households, as in that of Mr Glegg, in Ely, in 1549, where it was reported that 'much evil and incontinent living hath been had and used,' where

> three young women [had been] gotten with child within the space of one year … one woman to be with child by William Clarke's servant to Mr E. Glegg, and th'other to be with child already by Mr Glegg, which hath been corrected already … . There is another woman in Master Glegg's house lately come thither which is much suspected with Glegg, and the people be much offended and do talk very evil upon it because it is reported thar she commonly every night scratch his back, he being in bed.

When the case came before the church wardens, one woman was unwilling to accuse William Clarke, when 'her master Edward Glegg did say unto her that in case she would not lay the getting of the child to the said William's charge, he would thrust a pitchfork in her belly.'

Just occasionally, public shaming by exposure of illicit sex might be directed at a man, especially if he had some social status and reputation to lose – such as a priest. In 1586 a churchwarden reported, disapprovingly, how Ann Symes openly denounced a priest, John Lysby, at a vestry meeting:

> Being come in presence of Mr Lysby, the parson … she very boldly and shamefastly before the whole assembly began to accuse the said Mr Lysby in these words, viz., 'thou … hast most shamefully committed carnal copulation with me and hast occupied me divers and sundry times, as namely, twice in one Treale's house, a cook by Pie Corner, and there thou gavest money to the maid to keep the door while thou didst occupy me. And another time at the sign of The Black Lion without Bishopsgate, and divers other times since, thou hast had thy pleasure and use of me and in occupying me thou didst use me more ruffianlike than honestly.' All which words were spoken by the said Ann

Symes very boldly and without blushing or any shame at
all or womanlike modesty.

One can only wonder what lay behind this public humiliation. Lysby
'earnestly denied it and wished the ground might open under him if
the accusation of Ann Symes were true.' He continued in post, despite
some unease in his congregation, but was again 'defamed' by another
parishioner the following year.[4]

One modern writer thinks that 'occupy' was used euphemistically by
a prudish clerk of the court, but it is clear that it was normal usage, by all
classes, as is suggested by an epigram by the courtier Sir John Harington:

> Lesbia doth laugh to hear sellers and buyers
> Called by this name, Substantial occupiers;
> Lesbia, the word was good while good folk used it,
> You marred it, that with Chaucer's jest abused it:
> But good or bad, how e'er the word be made,
> Lesbia is loth to leave the trade.[5]

Doll Tearsheet uses it in *Henry IV, Part II*: 'The word occupy ... was an
excellent good word before it was ill sorted.'

Another priest, George Barton (apparently a repeat offender), had a
worse time of it, in 1563, as recorded in the City records:

> The 26 of June was a minister, a parson of Saint Mary
> Abchurch of St Martin's in Ironmonger Lane and other
> benefice ... taken at Distaff Lane using another man's wife
> as his own, which was the daughter to Sir Miles Partridge
> and wife to William Stokebregge, grocer, he being taken
> in the deed (having a wife of his own), was carried to
> Bridewell through all the streets, his breech hanging above
> his knees, his gown and hat borne after him ... but he lay
> not long there but was delivered without punishment and
> still enjoyed his benefices. They were greatly blamed that
> committed him.[6]

Once again, one wonders what went on; curiouser and curiouser, said Alice.

Apart from such remarkable instances, common-place adultery was usually punished by public shaming, as with Ursula Shepherd in 1589, when she had to attend Sunday service in church and declare:

> Good people, I do here, before God and you all, confess that whereas I have been married wife to Henry Shepherd for the space of twenty years I, forgetting God and my duty unto my husband, have committed adultery and played the harlot with one Richard Matthew my servant now of late time. And for the same I am by order of law divorced [separated] from my husband and enjoined to do this my penance. And therefore I desire you all to take example by me and I promise hereafter to lead a chaste life.

Public denunciations before the Church court were intended to satisfy the claimant by public shaming; the complainant might not always be a victim, but one ostensibly speaking on the assumption that unapproved sex was something of general public and local concern (or it might just have been out of malice or resentment). In crowded Elizabethan housing, especially in London, there was little privacy. One Judith Wright was prosecuted for 'defaming' – that is, exposing – her former mistress, by telling people that

> upon a time when [the husband] was at Bristol fair, I coming from market and going into an upper room in his house did see my mistress ... lying backward upon a settle with her coat turned up to her belly and that I did see her belly naked and one Master Hall leaning between her legs.

The court considered this defamation; the truth of her statement did not come into question. In any case, it was as well to keep on good terms with the servants.

Difficulties with servants could arise higher up the social scale (where enforced marriages might have had something to do with it). In 1566, a Somerset gentleman, Sir John Stawell, found his wife Mary being bedded by the servant John Stalling. Despite Sir John's reproofs, the affair continued and Mary became pregnant, before inducing a miscarriage. At last, when she started taking on other men servants,

Sir John acted, asking first the Bishop of Bath and Wells and then the Archbishop of Canterbury to be allowed to remarry, despite being already married to Mary. He was allowed a judicial separation and in 1572 was granted a licence to marry. Legal counteraction from Mary's family and other legal problems ensued, until a financial settlement bought them off from opposing Sir John's marriage with Frances Dyer, which eventually produced a son and heir.[7]

Another story of a surprisingly promiscuous upper-class wife was told by John Aubrey, of the wife of John Overall (1560–1618), Dean and Professor of St Paul's, and a translator of the Authorized Version of the Bible. Aubrey reports that she was 'the greatest beauty of her time in England.' He continues:

> She was not more beautiful than she was obliging and kind, and was so tender-hearted that (truly) she could scarce deny anyone. She had (they told me) the loveliest eyes that ever were seen, but wondrous wanton. When she came to Court, or to the play-house, the gallants would so flock about her .... .
>
> The good old Dean, notwithstanding that he knew well enough that he was horned, loved her infinitely: in so much that he was willing she should enjoy what she had a mind to.
>
> Among others who were charmed by her was Sir John Selby, of Yorkshire. Old Mistress Tyndale, who knew her, remembers a song made of her and Sir John, part whereof was this, viz:

> > The Dean of Paul's did search for his wife,
> >   and where d'ee think he found her?
> > Even upon Sir John Selby's bed,
> >   as flat as any flounder.

Aubrey goes on to quote a charming pastoral poem about her beauty and general amorous enthusiasm, concluding with lamenting her end:

> But gone she is, the prettiest lass
>   that ever trod on plain.
> Whatever hath betide of her,
>   blame not the shepherd swain.

For why? she was her owne foe,
    and gave herself the overthrow
By being so frank of her
    hye nonny nonny no.

* * * * *

Into a Blissful Paradise

Another instance of the upper-class wife and, in this case, gentleman servant guest, comes in George Gascoigne's story of an affair in a gentleman's house, *A Discourse of the Adventures passed by Master F. J.* (1573). Whilst fiction, it is the kind of thing that could have happened to Thomas Whythorne:

> Suppertime came and passed over, and not long after came the handmaid of the Lady Elinor into the great chamber, desiring F. J. to repair unto their mistress, the which he willingly accomplished; and being now entered into her chamber, he might perceive his mistress in her night's attire, preparing herself toward bed; to whom F. J. said, 'Why, how now, Mistress? I had thought this night to have seen you dance, at least or at last, amongst us.'
>
> 'By my troth, good servant,' quoth she, 'I adventured so soon unto the great chamber yesternight, that I find myself somewhat sickly disposed, and therefore do strain courtesy, as you see, to go the sooner to my bed this night; but before I sleep,' quoth she, 'I am to charge you with a matter of weight,' and taking him apart from the rest, declared that, as at that present night, she would talk with him more at large in the gallery adjoining her chamber. Hereupon F. J., discreetly dissimulating his joy, took his leave and retired into the great chamber, where he had not long continued before the Lord of the castle commanded a torch to light him to his lodging, whereas he prepared himself and went to bed, commanding his servant also to go to his rest.
>
> And when he thought his servant as the rest of the household be safe, he arose again, and taking his nightgown,

did under the same convey his naked sword, and so walked to the gallery, where he found his good mistress walking in her nightgown and attending his coming. The moon was now at the full, the skies clear, and the weather temperate, by reason whereof he might the more plainly, and with the greater contentation, behold his long desired joys, and spreading his arms abroad to embrace his loving mistress, he said, 'Oh my dear lady, when shall I be able with the least desert to countervail the least part of this your bountiful goodness?'

The dame (whether it were of fear indeed, or that the wiliness of womanhood had taught her to cover her conceits with some fine dissimulation) start back from the knight, and shrieking (but softly) said unto him, 'Alas, servant, what have I deserved, that you come against me with naked sword as against an open enemy?'

F. J., perceiving her intent, excused himself, declaring that he brought the same for their defence, and not to offend her in any wise. The lady being therewith somewhat appeased, they began with more comfortable gesture to expel the dread of the said late affright, and sithence to become bolder of behaviour, more familiar in speech, and most kind in accomplishing of common comfort. But why hold I so long discourse in describing the joys which (for lack of like experience) I cannot set out to the full? Were it not that I know to whom I write, I would the more beware what I write. F. J. was a man, and neither of us are senseless, and therefore I should slander him (over and besides a greater obloquy to the whole genealogy of Aeneas) if I should imagine that of tender heart he would forbear to express her more tender limbs against the hard floor.

Suffice that of her courteous nature she was content to accept boards for a bed of down, mats for cambric sheets, and the nightgown of F. J. for a counterpoint to cover them; and thus with calm content, instead of quiet sleep, they beguiled the night, until the proudest star began to abandon the firmament, when F. J. and his mistress were constrained also to abandon their delights, and with ten thousand sweet kisses and straight embracings, did frame themselves to play loth to depart. Well, remedy was there none, but Dame Elinor must return to her chamber, and F. J. must also convey himself, as closely as might be, into his chamber, the which was hard to do, the day being so far sprung, and he having a large base court to pass over before he could recover his stairfoot door. And though he were not much perceived, yet the Lady Frances being no less desirous to see an issue to these enterprises than F. J. was to cover them for secrecy, did watch, and even at the entering of his chamber door perceived the point of his naked sword glistering under the skirt of his nightgown; whereat she smiled and said to herself, 'This gear goeth well about.'

Well, F. J. having now recovered his chamber, he went to bed, and there let him sleep, as his mistress did on the other side. Although the Lady Frances, being thoroughly tickled now in all the veins, could not enjoy such quiet rest, but, arising, took another gentlewoman of the house with her, and walked into the park to take the fresh air of the morning.

There was always the danger of lively young men exploiting their position as guests or visitors in the household, as several facetious verses suggested. In one of John Donne's pieces, he casts himself as a successful seducer of a married woman, whom he has trained sexually as a lover:

> Nature's lay idiot, I taught thee to love,
> And in that sophistry, oh, thou dost prove
> Too subtle …
> Thou art not by so many duties his   [the husband]
> That from the world's common having severed thee,
> Inlaid thee, neither to be seen or see,
> As mine, who have with amorous delicacies
> Refined thee into a blissful paradise

Now, however, in a neat twist, he fears that he has taught her so well, that she will be unfaithful to him as well, with others:

Thy graces and good words my creatures be;
I planted knowledge and life's tree in thee,
Which, oh, shall strangers taste?

Of course, F. J. might not have been the first, or last, with Dame Elinor.

* * * * *

Occupiers

Men tended not to make public complaints and accusations of wives' adultery (unless, as was the case with Sir John Stawell, there were titles and estates to be protected), partly because they were supposed to be able to control them, and it reflected on their social status; no-one wanted to be known as a cuckold. Remarkably, when wives complained, their accusations were often directed at the other woman as much as at the husband. For example, in 1579, Alice Amos was a near neighbour of Richard and Susan Symonds in Boar Head Alley, off Fleet Street, when she called out of her window to Susan, 'Thou art a whore. And I saw my husband stand between thy legs and thou didst put thy hand into his codpiece very rudely.' Alice's husband himself called out, 'Remember the quart of cream, remember the quart of cream. Yea, thou art a whore indeed for I did occupy thee myself six times, for one mess of cream.' Clearly, he was not worried – the tomcat who had got the cream.[8]

Likewise, Agnes Seare, a carman's wife, complained at the bawdy court of her husband and Alice Leland: 'Thou hast occupied her ... round about the house. And thou hast occupied her as often as thou hast occupied me.' She told the court official:

> She ... is an harlot and my husband hath spent £40 pound on her. Her brother ... came home to my husband's house when my husband and I were at variance, and then he said to my husband, 'Let thy wife alone and come home to me and I will give thee £10 and a horse and cart with my sister' .... I have called her a whore any time these five years and yet I will stand to it.

When a wife could not stop her husband's affair, she would attack her rival, saying she was a whore. Thus Alice Rochester called Jane Lilham 'a whore, an arrant whore, and a common carted whore ... . My husband hath kept thee a great while at Newcastle and all that he got he spent on thee. Thou hast lain oftener with him than he hath done with me.' Elizabeth Hodgkins had a warrant served on the other woman, crying, 'Now I have thee, whore,' describing her as 'the bastard-bearing whore who hath made my husband spend ten pounds on her since Lent began'. All the woman's fault, the husband not blamed. When Elizabeth Frier found her husband drinking with Margaret Yard in a tavern in Turnbull Street (a notorious area for brothels and whores), she struck her, saying, 'Thou art Stephen Yard's wife but thou art my husband's whore. He can be contented to spend ten shillings on thee but he will not spend two pence in my company.'

The location in this incident might be significant: quite a few dissatisfied men turned, not to adultery but to professionals. As mentioned earlier, there were many brothels near Clerkenwell, such as Turnmill, or Turnbull, Street, with adjacent squalid alleys, or Pickthatch (the 'hatch' was a metal grille set in the heavily barred doors of houses, especially brothels). Justice Shallow, in *Henry IV, Part II*, boasted of 'the feats he hath done about Turnbull Street', when a young law student. In 1592, Henry Chettle, in *Kinde Hartes Dreame*, wrote of Turnmill Street where landlords charged

> forty shillings yearly for a little Room with a smoky chimny ... where several of these venereal virgins are resident, [subject] to suche fynes, suche tributes, suche customes as poore Soules, after seven years Service in that unhallowed Order they are fayne to leave ... seekynge harboure in an hospital.

* * * * *

The Expense of Spirit

Of course, not all adulteries were just occasional, brief, bit-of-fun-on-the-side encounters, but long-lasting, serious and emotionally involved relationships (such as that of Simon Forman and Avisa Allen), producing their own stresses and dissatisfactions, as in the case of married William Shakespeare and his anonymous married 'Dark Lady of the Sonnets'.

The affair does not appear to have brought them much contentment; several sonnets outline the course of the relationship, expressing increasing bitterness. In *Sonnet 142* he writes, admitting his own falsity, and suggesting hers:

> Love is my sin, and thy dear virtue hate,
> Hate of my sin, grounded on sinful loving;
> O, but with mine compare thou thine own state,
> And thou shalt find it merits not reproving;
> Or, if it do, not from those lips of thine,
> That have profaned their scarlet ornaments
> And sealed false bonds of love as oft as mine,
> Robbed others' beds revenues of their rents …

The writer's profound disgust with compulsive sexual activity is expressed most powerfully and bitterly, in *Sonnet 129*: 'Th'expense of spirit in a waste of shame / Is lust in action … / Enjoyed no sooner but despised straight … /A bliss in proof, and proved, a very woe,/ Before, a joy proposed, behind, a dream.' Fortunately, not all Shakespeare's extra-marital episodes were serious. There is the famous story, told by John Manningham, a law student, who noted it in 1602, of how:

> Upon a time when [Richard] Burbage played Richard III, there was a citizen grew so far in liking with him, that before she went from the play she appointed him to come that night to her by the name of Richard the Third. Shakespeare, overhearing their conversation, went before, was entertained at his game ere Burbage came. Then, message being brought that Richard the Third was at the door, Shakespeare caused return to be made that William the Conqueror was before Richard the Third.

It would be nice if it were true.

Another, very different story of a long-lasting, unsatisfactory relationship, is that of a young maidservant, seduced by a married friend of her employers, and the determined efforts made by her mistress to help her. Susan More lived as a servant with a bookseller, Randall Berk, and his wife, Anne, near Cripplegate, working on silk ribbons and points (laces). One day, a printer, Thomas Creede, visited on business and 'began to praise the handsomeness of Susan More', saying, 'Randall, thou hast gotten a pretty wench to thy maid here. I would I could be acquainted with her. I will give her a pint of wine for that she is so like my first wife.' At first she declined, but eventually he persuaded the Berks to go with her to The King's Head, in Redcross Street. The next morning, Susan told Anne that Creede had promised her he would come again, and 'give her as good a breakfast as ever she had in all her life.' Despite Anne's warnings, later that day Susan slipped away to The King's Head, where Anne found her with Creede. She berated them both, telling Creede that 'it was neither fit nor credit for him or any other married man to sit spending his money with a young maid in a tavern', and criticising Susan for neglecting her work.

Susan continued to get away to meet her experienced admirer, and, that summer, at the Sun Tavern in Aldersgate, she became drunk and sick. Creede took her to 'one Widow Grimes's house, by Pickthatch, an alehouse, and led her up to a chamber where she … lay down on a bed to sleep, and she sayeth that at that time the same Thomas Creede had the carnal knowledge of her body.' He persuaded her to continue meeting him at Widow Grimes's house, when she became pregnant. She told Creede, who said that as she had stayed with the Berks, he would have nothing to do with her, saying, 'I will shift it off, and my wife will help to clear me of this matter and to shift it off, as she has shifted me off such matters as this before now.'

Susan asked the Berks' kitchen maid to plead with him, but he continued to reject her, saying she 'should not gull him neither would he be gulled of her nor her mother neither'. At last, Susan told her mistress, Anne Berk, who told her off: 'Of late when Mistress Worrall [a neighbour] and my husband fell out and called you "whore" and "Creede's whore" for it, did not you then deny all such matters?' When Randall Berk went to Creede, he denied it all: 'Doth she say so? Well you know, Master Berk, if a whore will swear a child upon a man he must keep it and so must I belike, but sure if it be mine, she is something big.'

It was then agreed that they would all meet at the Sun Tavern. There, as Anne reported, Mistress Creede advanced on Susan 'with a very fierce and angry countenance', demanding, 'Are you with child by my husband?' Susan fell on her knees and begged for forgiveness. Then Creede's wife threatened her that if she would not find another father for her child, she would have her to Bridewell, and have her whipped every court day and work all the week, and she [Mrs Creede] would have the benefit of her work and keep her with brown bread and water, and so in such terrible threatening manner terrified the wench as much as she could.

Anne then brought about a calmer mood, when it was decided that Susan would go to stay with friends in Cambridge, and Mrs Creede gave her ten shillings, Berk six more on Creede's account, and Anne one shilling and sixpence. The two wives then escorted Susan to the Cambridge carrier at The Bull in Bishopsgate, while Susan told them more about Creede at Widow Grimes's house: 'he used to have other women besides her there, as namely one from Lambeth, another that had a great belly, and a third that was there ... but she being now something old she said that he had told her that he cared not for her now.' After this, Susan did not get to Cambridge after all, but, in the bitter winter cold of early January, she could not endure the jolting of the wagon, and came back. Rather than try the Berks, she stayed in 'one old Mother Cop's house' for five nights, 'walked up and down the street for one night', and eventually found refuge in 'a poor woman's house in Gravel Lane in Houndsditch where she lay two days and two nights without meat or drink.'

When Anne found that Susan had come back to London, she told the Creedes, who were angry, and Creede said that he would not be 'gulled'. Anne then found Susan and got two women witnesses to interrogate her. She kept to her story, convinced them, and was then persuaded to have Creede 'to be called before some Justice, and then he would take some order for her.' At first, the justice, Sir Stephen Soane, was inclined to believe Creede, but after questioning Susan he changed his mind, bound Creede over to the next sessions, and ordered him to pay Susan's expenses for one month before and one month after her delivery.

Anne persuaded Susan to stay with a couple of Anne's friends in town while she lay in, the Creedes paying all charges. Soane insisted that the birth be supervised by a neutral midwife; when the time came, the midwife and a neighbour were present and reported that Susan had 'in her greatest pain and extremity of childbirth did confess and acknowledge' that Creede was the father. After this, the Creedes had to take full responsibility for the child, putting it out to nurse in the country.

Susan was spared the Bridewell, and went to work in a stationer's. Creede was prosecuted for bastardy.[9]

What might actually have happened to the child is suggested by an episode in Thomas Heywood's early Jacobean play, *The Wisewoman of Hogsdon* (1604), where the eponymous bawd, midwife and helper of women in trouble, tells of 'kitchen maids, and chambermaids, and sometimes good men's daughters, who having caught a clap and growing near their time, get leave to see their friends in the country for a week or two … for leaving their brats behind them.' Asked 'what became of the poor infants,' she replies, 'Why, in the night we send them abroad, and lay one at this man's door, and another at that, such as are able to keep them; and what after becomes of them, we inquire not.'

One adulterous affair in Faversham, Kent, aroused widespread horror, as reported by John Stow in *Annales of England* (1605). In 1551, following a lengthy affair with a tailor, Thomas Mosby, 'a black, swart man', Alice Arden decided her husband, John Arden, had to be got rid of. After her bungled attempt to poison his breakfast, she got one John Grene to hire Black Will, 'a terrible ruffian', to murder John for £10 – a considerable sum. They resolved to kill him at home on – ironically – Valentine's Day. As Mosby and John Arden were playing at 'tables' (backgammon), Black Will emerged from a cupboard where he was hiding and strangled John with a towel; Mosby beat him on the head with a heavy iron and Will finished him off with a dagger. Alice made sure, by stabbing the body seven times. She then paid the £10, and Black Will rode off. Alice, Mosby and two helpful servants dragged the body into a nearby field, hoping the falling snow would hide the traces. That evening, like Lady Macbeth, she entertained some guests, but no ghost appeared.

The next day, she made anxious enquiries for her missing husband, and the mayor's search party soon found the body, with footprints leading back to the house. Alice and her servants, and then Mosby, all confessed. After the trial, they were all executed: Alice, a conniving female servant and Black Will were all burned. Mosby, his accomplice sister and a male servant were hanged, some in chains.

In 1592, a sensational domestic-murder tragedy, *Arden of Feversham*, appeared with innocent John, Lady Macbeth Alice, Mosby and two splendid, half-comic villains, Black Will and his sidekick Shakebag. It was a success (there have been suggestions that Shakespeare was involved), and it has been performed occasionally over the centuries, even quite recently.

Chapter 6

The Court

'Courts are upon earth the vainest places.'
Sir Henry Wotton (1568–1639)

Curious Wits and Courtly Nymphs

For all that the Court was, in principle, the pinnacle of civilisation, the magnet for those seeking power, influence and wealth – or merely to seduce – not everyone spoke well of it. Sir Walter Raleigh wrote that 'it glows and shines like rotten wood', and Donne asked:

> hast thou seen
> O sun, in all thy journey, vanity
> Such as swells the bladder of our Court?

There was more than one Court building. The chief palace, Whitehall, sprawled over some twenty-three acres, in an area roughly bounded (in today's geography) by Green Park to the west, Westminster Abbey and Hall to the south, the river to the east, and Charing Cross and Northumberland Avenue to the north. There were several other palaces in or near London, including the Tower, Bridewell (largely reduced to a prison or place of correction), Eltham, Richmond (a favourite of the Queen), Greenwich, Nonsuch, Hampton Court, Windsor, Westminster and St James. The Queen ruled over a royal household of more than 1,700 people of all ranks, from the great officers of State, and aristocrats and their wives and daughters, and Court preachers, to guards, hairdressers, ostlers and kitchen maids (one of whom was to be responsible for a disastrous fire in Charles II's time). There seemed to be innumerable minor courtiers and hangers-on, making the best of their positions and generally doing little good or harm. In his *Satire 4*,

105

Donne gives a shrewd account of a typical Court morning of flirting and feigning:

> 'Tis ten o'clock, and past; all whom the mews, [stables]
> Balloon, tennis, diet or the stews   [volley-ball, brothels]
> Had all the morning held, now the second
> Time made ready, that day, in flocks are found
> In the Presence, and I (God pardon me).
> As fresh and sweet their apparels be, as be
> The fields they sold to buy them … . Now
> The ladies come, as pirates which do know
> That there came weak ships fraught with
>   cochineal,   [used for cosmetics]
> The men board them, and praise, as they think, well,
> Their beauties; they the men's wits; both are bought …

Among the Queen's immediate women companion servants were three or four ladies of the bedchamber, who were members of the aristocracy; below them, a dozen ladies of the privy chamber, and then half a dozen or so maids of honour, who were teenage daughters of the aristocracy or upper gentry. The maids were to provide the Queen with pleasant company with chatting, music and singing, and to lose to her at cards or dice. (Ben Jonson reported that 'she always had about Christmas evens-set dice, that threw sixes or five, and she knew not they were other, to make her win and esteem herself fortunate.') They brightened the Court by day with youthful charm and gaiety, and spent their night in the Coffer Chamber, a sort of girls' dormitory; one can imagine what went on in there. One anecdote reports how 'the Maids of Honour used to frisk and hey about'; unfortunately, this was next to the apartment occupied by Vice-Chamberlain of the Household Sir Francis Knollys (c. 1514–1596), who was married to the Queen's cousin. He was annoyed by the late-night rumpus:

> though he had often warned them of it; at last he gets one to
> bolt their own back door, when they were all in one night at
> their revels, strips to his [night] shirt, and so with a pair of
> spectacles on his nose, and Aretino [the favourite pornographer

of the time, writer of sexually explicit sonnets, translated in 1570] in his hand, came marching in at the postern door of his very chamber, reading very gravely, full upon the faces of them. Now judge what a sad spectacle and pitiful fright these poor creatures endured, for he faced them and often traversed the room in this posture about an hour.

Had he read them some moral tract – he was supposed to be somewhat puritanical – that would have been understandable; but to read these girls erotic verses almost constitutes a verbal sexual assault (perhaps substituting for a suppressed real one). Whilst they might have been abashed during this time, considerable – if smothered – giggling must have followed his departure.

The Queen, committed as she was to celibacy, order and rule, was not an easy mistress, especially as she got older while her maids apparently stayed much the same age, and was notoriously resentful and jealous of their – carefully subdued – love lives. They were there on their own account, to attract future husbands, and were themselves the prey of the men. As immediate servants of the Queen, they could not marry without her permission and this was not always readily granted. Sir John Harington reported one instance of her hostility to others' amorous wishes:

She did oft ask the ladies around her chamber if they loved to think of marriage, and the wise ones did conceal well their liking thereto, as knowing the Queen's judgement in this matter. Sir Matthew Arundel's fair cousin, not knowing so deeply as her fellows, was asked one day hereof, and simply said she had thought much about marriage, if her father did consent to the man she loved. 'You seem honest, i'faith,' said the Queen, 'I will sue for you to your father.' The damsel was not displeased hereat; and when Sir Robert came to Court, the Queen asked him hereon, and pressed his consenting, if the match was discreet. Sir Robert, much astonished at this news, said he never heard his daughter had liking to any man, and wanted to gain knowledge of her affection, but would give free consent to what was most pleasing to her Highness's will and advice. 'Then I will do the rest,' saith the Queen. The lady was called in, and the Queen told her her father had given his free consent. 'Then,' replied the lady, 'I shall be happy, and please your Grace.' 'So thou shalt, but not to be a fool and marry. I have his consent given to me, and I vow thou shalt never get it into thy possession. So go to thy business, I see thou art a bold one to own thy foolishness so readily.'

Naturally, there was a lot of yearning and flirtation, out of the Queen's knowledge. In October 1591 Richard Brackenbury wrote to Robert, second Earl of Essex (1566–1601), favourite of the Queen and dashing man-about-Court, who was away commanding forces sent to help Henri IV in Normandy, about how quiet life at Court was without him. He added that, 'ladies and gentlemen, not respecting the honour of war nor the public good, wisheth your lordship at home, saying a man of such a personage should be here in England.' Despite him saying that 'love here is almost banished', flirtation seems to have been very active. 'My cousin … sighs if Mistress Acton be but once named. Mistress Ansley hath not yet found the way to love, though there be good schoolmasters. What sports we had in the [Queen's] progress my brother Darcy can report, for he saw the best.' He goes on to say that if the Kingsmill sisters come to Court, 'they must learn to abide shot of all sorts, for at the return of so many soldiers the wars will grow dangerous.'

He was to prove prophetic, as the 1590s were to see an extraordinary number of irregular liaisons, notorious affairs and sudden marriages, driven partly by the influx of returning young men, feeling full of themselves after their military exploits. This is much the situation at the beginning of *Much Ado About Nothing* (1598), with Claudio returning from having had a good war, and now with an eye on Hero, saying that before he went to war, he had

> looked upon her with a soldier's eye
> That liked, but had a rougher task in hand …
> But now I am returned, and that war-thoughts
> Have left their places vacant, in their rooms
> Come thronging soft and delicate desires,
> All prompting me how fair young Hero is.

They marry with their parents' permission but without sufficient thought; and it does not turn out well.

Marrying without the Queen's consent could carry severe penalties, even if the parents had approved. The widowed Countess of Rutland transferred the care of her 11-year-old daughter, Bridget, to the Duchess of Bedford, who decided to send the little girl to Court, where in 1589 she became a maid of honour and developed into a recognised Court beauty, praised in verse by Barnabe Barnes. The countess wanted to marry Bridget to Sir Robert Tyrwhitt of Lincolnshire, with a view to easing a quarrel between the two families, and so brought her back to the family home at Belvoir Castle. At 16, Bridget was agreeable to the idea, as was Sir Robert, and the couple was duly married in 1594 – but in secret and without the necessary approval of the Queen, who had been told that Bridget was at home suffering from the measles. Soon, however, the marriage was discovered; the Queen was very angry, and, despite grovelling and pleading, the newly-weds were ordered to return to Court, when they were separated by royal command, and Tyrwhitt sent to prison. Eventually the Queen relented, and the marriage was approved. They had four children, and Bridget died in 1604.

In the enclosed, hot-house atmosphere of the Court world, the spoilt teenage maids were constantly falling in love with, and falling out with, the conceited young aristocrats surrounding them, who did not always take them seriously (even when taking them). Among the more notable figures at Court was Edward de Vere (1550–1604), the 17th Earl of Oxford, made a ward of Lord Burghley until he was of age. The scholar and writer, Gabriel Harvey, no admirer, described him and his dress (which came first):

> Strait to the back, like a shirt, and close to the breech like a diveling;
>
> A little apish hat, couched fast to the pate, like an oyster;
>
> French cambric cuffs, deep with a witness, starched to the purpose;
>
> Delicate in speech; quaint in array; conceited in all points;
>
> In courtly guiles, a passing singular odd man.

Obviously conceited (in the modern sense), a talented musician and dancer – which won him the Queen's favour – temperamental, quarrelsome and sharp of tongue, he caused a flutter among the sillier young maids. He wrote a verse with them particularly in mind:

> If women could be fair, and yet not fond,
> Or that their loves were firm, not fickle still,
> I would not wonder that they make men bond,
> Or service long to purchase their good will.
>> But when I see how frail these creatures are,
>> I muse that men forget themselves so far.
> To make the choice they make, and how they change,
> How oft from Phoebus they do cleave to Pan,
> Unsettled still, like haggards wild they range,   [half-trained hawks]
> These gentle birds, that fly from man to man.
>> Who would not scorn, and shake them from the fist,
>> And let me go, fair fools, which way they list.
> Yet for disport, we fawn and flatter both,
> To pass the time, when nothing else can please.
> And train them to our lure with subtle oath,
> Till, weary of our wills, ourselves we ease.
> And then we say, when we their fancies try,
> To play with fools, O what a dolt was I.

For all that, in 1571 a Court commentator wrote that Oxford

> hath gotten him a wife – or at least a wife hath caught him. That is Mistress Anne Cecil [favourite daughter of Lord Burghley], whereunto the Queen hath given her consent, the which hath caused great weeping, wailing and sorrowful cheer, of those that had hoped to have had that golden day. Thus you may see, whilst that some triumph with olive branches, others follow the chariot with willow gardens [wreaths].

The others were luckier than they knew. In fact, neither the Queen nor Burghley was pleased with this, and almost immediately he went abroad, returning in 1576 as a Catholic, 'a great spender', it was noted, and estranged from his wife and Burghley (whom he blamed for not having prevented the execution of the Duke of Norfolk in 1572). John Aubrey has a memorable story of him: 'The Earl of Oxford, making of his low obeisance to Queen Elizabeth, happened to let a fart, at which he was so abashed and ashamed that he went to travel, seven years. On his return the Queen welcomed him home, and said, "My Lord, I had forgot the fart."'

He had a famous quarrel with Philip Sidney in the Whitehall tennis court in 1579, when the Queen had to remind Sidney of the deference due to an earl. Next year, he had an affair with Anne Vavasour (born c. 1565, former gentlewoman of the bedchamber), who in March 1581 actually gave birth 'in the Maidens' chamber'. She and Oxford were promptly sent to the Tower (though in 1595 it was suggested that the Earl of Essex was the father). He was released in June, on condition that he return to his wife, which went so far as her rapidly giving birth to four children before her death in 1588 (Burghley providing a home and support for her family). In 1582 he had to fight a duel with her cousin, Thomas Knyvett (who, in 1605, was to find Guy Fawkes under the House of Lords), which was followed by brawls between his and Knyvett's followers, some of whom were killed. He took part in the Flanders campaign in 1585, and married again, another maid of honour, who bore him a son. He was active in the drama; some people like to think of him as writing Shakespeare's plays, despite dying in 1604.

* * * * *

Pretty Maids All in a Row

As for Anne Vavasour, after the death in 1590 of the wife of Sir Henry Lee ('Queen's Champion' at the Royal Tilts, whom gossip reported a son of Henry VIII), she settled as his mistress, living with him at Charlbury and Ditchley in Oxfordshire. On his death, she married a Mr John Finch. Her sister, Frances, also (as they say) 'put it about a bit' at Court, where in November 1590, it was said she 'flourisheth like the lily and the rose' (whatever that may mean), before becoming mistress of Robert Dudley (1574–1649), illegitimate son of the Earl of Leicester and his mistress, Lady Douglas Sheffield (c. 1544–1608), then herself the wife of Lord Sheffield, whom she had married when she was 17, before going on to marry Edward Stafford in 1579. Frances had expected to marry Robert: there was an espousal in 1591, which was even approved by the Queen, who said, perhaps wisely, that they should wait until Robert was a little older. Frances was not prepared to risk that, and instead shrewdly – and in secret – married Sir Thomas Shirley (who had himself recently been courting the dowager Lady Stourton). The usual banishment from Court ensued, and Shirley did time in Marshalsea Prison. As for Dudley, in that year he was 'commanded from the Court for kissing mistress [Margaret] Cavendish in the Presence Chamber', whom he then married. In 1596 he took part in the Cadiz raid, and was knighted, as were too many. Margaret having died, he then married Alice Leigh, daughter of the wealthy merchant and former Lord Mayor of London, Sir Thomas Leigh, who gave the couple Kenilworth Castle.

Sir Thomas may have encouraged Sir Robert to reopen the question of his legitimacy. The case, opposed by Lettice, daughter of Sir Francis Knollys, dowager Countess of Leicester and mother of the Earl of Essex, who had also wanted Kenilworth, went to the Star Chamber in 1605, when Sir Robert lost and was charged £100. Now, disgusted with this, a Catholic convert and at a time of anti-Catholic feeling, he eloped with Elizabeth Southwell (1586–1631), a maid of honour and his cousin and latest mistress, to France; Elizabeth was disguised as his pageboy, rather like Jessica in *The Merchant of Venice*, and the couple in Donne's poem, *On his Mistress* (which actually refers to his young wife). In that poem, the speaker is travelling abroad and warns her not to accompany him dressed as a pageboy, as 'men of France, changeable chameleons ... will quickly know thee, and know thee, and alas / Th'indifferent Italian ... well content to think thee page / Will haunt thee, with such lust.' The poem was probably written in about 1602; perhaps Dudley knew it. At any rate, the couple was accepted as Catholics and soon acquired a papal dispensation to marry. In Florence, Dudley did well, gaining wealth and the title of Duke of Northumberland, and they went on to have thirteen children. Henry, Prince of Wales, bought Kenilworth, and Alice, left behind, became duchess in 1645.

One of the more remarkable, even notorious, careers of a maid of honour was that of Mary Fitton (1578–1647), daughter of Sir Edward Fitton of Cheshire. When it was thought time to send her up to Court, Sir Edward wrote to Sir William Knollys (c. 1547–1632), son of Sir Francis, comptroller and later treasurer of the Household, married to Dorothy Bridges, widow of Lord Chandos and some years older than himself, and asked Sir William to protect her in the dangerous jungle of the Court. Sir William reported on 'the wolfish cruelty and fox-like subtlety of the tame beasts in this place, which when they seem to take bread at a man's hand will bite before they will bark; all their songs be siren-like and their tears are after Judas fashion.' With this in mind, he assured

Sir Edward that he would be 'as careful of her well-doing as if I were her true father' (his own marriage was childless). His grand position at Court enabled him to get her a position as a favoured maid of honour; she was even allowed to ride one of the Queen's horses and be known as Bay Fitton. There could have been suggestive jokes about her riding; 'bay', while referring to the horse's colour, could also have other innuendos: a Shakespeare sonnet refers to a promiscuous woman as 'the bay where all men ride', and Othello is to 'bless this bay with his tall ship, /Make love's quick pants in Desdemona's arms' and Donne uses 'embayed' to suggest where the lover would wish to be.

At 17, Mary was attractive and lively, and Sir William, aged 48, became infatuated with her, even hopefully dyeing his beard, to widespread derision. It is suggested that he was the model for Malvolio in *Twelfth Night* (1601–2), the Italian words *male voglia*, 'badly desire' modulating into Malvoglio, 'I want Mall (Mary)'. However, Mary was more interested in younger men, especially William Herbert (1580–1630), later third Earl of Pembroke. He first went to Court in 1597, and London the following year, and, despite his more sober later years, had been having a high old time. Lord Clarendon later wrote that he had 'indulged to himself the pleasures of all kinds, almost in all excess'. He may have paid a penalty for this, in that he was almost certainly infected with the pox; he later smoked a lot of tobacco, then thought of as medicinal and effective against syphilis, so his infection may not have been recognised at the time.

William's parents, the Pembrokes, had been trying for some time to get him married and settled (some have suggested that the Shakespeare sonnets urging a young man to marry had him in mind). In 1595, the Earl tried to marry him to Elizabeth Carey, granddaughter of Lord Hunsdon, but William was not willing; Elizabeth promptly married Sir Thomas Berkeley, who soon spent all their money before dying at 37. Then, in 1597, they tried to get Lord Burghley's daughter, Bridget Vere, but that fell through over dowry and annuity disputes. The following year saw them disappointed of Elizabeth Hatton, the 20-year-old daughter of Sir Thomas Cecil; in 1598, a wealthy widow, she married the 47-year-old widower, Sir Edward Coke, the Queen's attorney (gossip said that, ten weeks after the wedding, she gave birth, reputedly begotten of a servant).

By now, Mary Fitton had definitely set her cap at William Herbert, and pursued him with vigour – literally: running to visit him at the family home at Baynard's Castle, by the river, her hair hidden under a hood, and wearing a long white cloak with her skirts tucked up, hoping to be taken for a man. Sir William Knollys was sadly out of the running. A doggerel verse went around (original spelling):

> partie beard was aferd
> when they ran at the heard
> the Raine deer was imbost
> the white doe she was loste
> Pembroke stroke her downe
> and took her from the clowne
> Lord for thy pittie

The clown with the partly coloured beard was obviously Knollys, distressed when 'they' – the young courtiers – chased the herd of maids of honour, seeing Mary as the doe and himself with the antlered horns of a cuckold (and 'embossed': either foaming at the mouth or with the round bosses of disease swellings) by young Pembroke.

They both attended a great celebration in June 1600, for the wedding of Lady Anne Russell, a former maid of honour, to another Herbert, Henry, Lord Herbert of Chepstow. It was all very grand and splendid, in the presence of the Queen; when Mary took part in an allegorical dance in a masque before the Queen, she was asked, what she represented, and replied, 'Affection'. 'Affection?' harrumphed the Queen, 'Affection's false.' However, 67-year-old Elizabeth did get up and join the dance. Things may have been going too well for the young couple, for in spring 1601 Mary was visibly pregnant. He admitted being responsible, but refused to marry her, and was sent to Fleet Prison. The child was stillborn. It is possible that he had infected her: both complained of feeling unwell, he of an 'ague', she, ironically, of 'the mother', an unspecified condition. It has been suggested that William Clowes, the Queen's physician, had been consulted when Mary was in the custody of Lady Hawkins, and could then have diagnosed syphilis, which would have further angered the Queen.

He was eventually released and went on with his career abroad and in London, supporting the theatre and patronising poets. From 1617 he was Chancellor of Oxford University (Pembroke College was named for him), and gave many books and manuscripts to Sir Thomas Bodley's Library, outside which his bronze statue by Hubert Le Sueur still stands. In 1623, Heminges and Condell dedicated the Shakespeare First Folio to him and his brother. Before that, in 1604, he married Mary Talbot, a daughter of the Earl of Shrewsbury, described as very short and very plain, but very wealthy; the marriage was childless. Clarendon remarked that 'he paid much too dear for his wife's fortune by taking her person into the bargain'. Presumably he carried on in his accustomed fashion, as Clarendon went on, 'he was immoderately given up to women'.

As for Mary, she had to go back to her embarrassed parents in Cheshire for a while; Sir William Knollys was still, like Barkis, willing, but she would not have him. When his wife died in 1605, Sir William waited for two months before, at the age of 68, marrying Elizabeth Howard, aged 19, daughter of the Earl of Suffolk. She bore two sons, in 1627 and 1631, neither of whom he acknowledged or bequeathed anything. He did well at Court under James I, becoming a baron, a Knight of the Garter and eventually Earl of Banbury (so Mary could have become a countess, had she wished), before dying at the age of 83. Mary herself went on to become mistress to Vice-Admiral Sir Richard Leveson, unfortunately already married; when he died prematurely in 1605, he left her all of £100. Another sailor now hove into view, Captain William Polwhele, a Cornishman and commander of a pinnace named *Lion's Whelp*. After she bore him a son, they got married, and then she had a daughter. Her mother was never reconciled to her wayward daughter's irregularities, lamenting in a letter, 'such shame as never had a Cheshire woman, worse now than ever'. The captain died in 1610, but then there was yet another naval husband, a Welshman, Captain Lougher. He lived until 1636, and Mary died in 1647, aged 75, and is buried in Gawsworth, in Cheshire.

One maid of honour who earned the unremitting hostility of the Queen was Elizabeth Throckmorton (1565–1647), who went up to Court in 1584. Although not a great heiress – her father had left her a portion of £500, which the Earl of Huntingdon borrowed and never repaid, she was sought after, notably by the dashing, very masculine Sir Walter Raleigh (c. 1552–1618), himself much favoured by the Queen who, as Aubrey remarked, 'loved to have all the servants of her Court proper men'; he was quite capable of laying his cloak at the Queen's feet, as legend relates. He had cut something of a swathe through the Court's young ladies. Aubrey recorded a famous anecdote, presumably reported by Sir Walter himself:

> He loved a wench well; and one time getting up one of the Mayds of Honour up against a tree in a Wood ('twas his first Lady) who seemed at first boarding to be something fearfull of her Honour, and modest, she cryed, 'Sweet Sir Walter, what doe you me ask? Will you undoe me? Nay, sweet Sir Walter! Sweet Sir Walter! Sir Walter!' At last, as the danger and the pleasure at the same time grew higher, she cryed in the extasey, 'Swisser Swatter Swisser Swatter'. She proved with child, and I doubt not but this Hero tooke care of them both.

There is no record of what actually happened to the ruined girl. There is one problem with Aubrey's story: she was unlikely to be 'his first lady', as he was knighted in 1585, when he was around 33 (unless Aubrey's phrasing is intended to discount any of her non-aristocratic predecessors).

Now, in 1590, at the age of around 38, he fell for Elizabeth, aged about 27, herself very mature for a maid of honour. A secret marriage ensued, and a son was born in London, who died in infancy. She went back to Court, while he was busy with preparations for an expedition against the Spanish; the fleet had barely sailed before the Queen demanded his return. The Queen was predictably furious at the news (probably from friends of his rival, the Earl of Essex), and Raleigh was in the Tower sometime that July. He was released in September, to deal with arrangements regarding the enormous loot from the captured Spanish carrack, the *Madre de Dios,* much of which was to go to the Queen. In December he retired from the Court to his Dorset home in Sherborne, and his (second) son Walter was baptised on 1 November 1593. The Queen never forgave Elizabeth for her misconduct (or stealing Raleigh), and an attempt in 1601 to reinstate her at Court failed. King James was always hostile to him; when Sir Walter was introduced to him, he said (according to Aubrey), 'O my soul, mon, I have heard rawly of thee.' From 1603 to 1616 he was held in the Tower. Lady Raleigh lived with him in the Tower most of the time until 1610, when she was ordered out to their house in London. After his execution in 1618, she was allowed to take home only his head, which she had embalmed.

* * * * *

Essex is Not the Way

Raleigh's chief enemy during Elizabeth's time was his rival, Robert Devereux, second Earl of Essex, son of Walter Devereux and Lettice Knollys (on Walter's death she promptly married Robert Dudley, Earl of Leicester, and then Sir Christopher Blount).

Lettice's four children by the first Earl of Essex, largely brought up by the Earl and Countess of Huntingdon, included Penelope (1563–1607) and Dorothy (1564–1619) Devereux, two golden-haired, black-eyed Court beauties. Having arrived at Court at the age of 17, in 1583 Dorothy got away from the Huntingdons and eloped, scandalously, with Sir Thomas Perrot, whom she had known since childhood (a later portrait shows her with a parrot). They ran off to the parish church at Broxbourne in Hertfordshire, bringing two armed guards to prevent any interruption by the Huntingdons. When asked for the keys of the church, the local priest refused to give them up, so they had to find another clergyman to conduct the service. The Queen was furious, as usual; Perrot did time in Fleet Prison, and she refused to speak to Dorothy even four years later. After Perrot's death, Dorothy married, in 1595, Henry Percy, (1564–1632), ninth Earl of Northumberland, though, as it turned out, not happily. They lived mostly at Petworth in Sussex, where his scientific experiments earned him the name of 'wizard'. He was involved, to some uncertain degree, in the Gunpowder Plot of 1605 – he always proclaimed his innocence – and was imprisoned in the Tower until 1621, where he managed to live in some state before returning to Petworth.

It was the elder sister, Penelope, who was to cause the greater stir in Court and literary circles. Although, in 1576, the Huntingdons considered marrying her, at 13 or so, to Philip Sidney (22), Philip was not ready for this, and her father, Walter, died before the marriage could be arranged. Walter had thought highly of Philip, and would have liked her to marry him. When dying, he left a message for Philip: 'Tell him I send him nothing [he was described as the poorest earl in England – well, these things are relative], but I wish him well and so well that if God do move both their hearts I wish he might match with my daughter. He is wise, virtuous and godly. I call him son.' When it came to it, money, as so often, was the dealbreaker – the Sidneys needed more than was on offer – whilst Sir Henry Sidney did not like the earl and so was unlikely to be flexible in the matter. (Ironically, when Walter died in dubious circumstances in 1576, Sir Henry was deputed to lead the formal investigation.) Penelope was brought to Court in 1581, when the Huntingdons promptly married her off, very much against her will, to 'rich Lord Rich', whose only charm was his money, on 1 November.

The marriage never stood a chance. Though he had been to Cambridge University, he did not seem to have benefitted intellectually, but remained sullen and dull – and made duller by Puritanism – whilst Penelope was glamorous, lively, skilled in music and fluent in Italian and Spanish. They had little to do with each other, apart from her rare visits to Essex for impregnation to continue the Rich inheritance. She had a wide circle of friends and admirers interested in music and literature. The French Court lutenist dedicated his book of chansons to her, and the Italian lexicographer and writer, John Florio (an acquaintance of Shakespeare), dedicated his influential translation of Montaigne's *Essays* to her in 1603: 'truly richest Lady Rich, in riches of Fortune not deficient, but of body incomparably richer, of mind most rich'.

At some point, Philip Sidney apparently fell in love with her. Now, at 18 or so, in her full beauty, fascinating, intelligent, but married, she unintentionally provoked, in *Astrophil and Stella*, a sequence of 108 sonnets and other songs of idealised love and high-minded frustration, skilfully composed with wit and eloquence. The sequence, where Astrophil ('star-lover') is and is not Philip and Stella ('star') is and is not Penelope, was no autobiographical outpouring, but something more subtle. Its ambiguous nature is implicit in its first line: 'Loving in truth and fain in verse my love to show', where truth and faining (desiring) and feigning (pretending, fictionalising) are set against each other. Ostensibly a love story, it is in reality a poetic exploration of the current tensions between idealistic, Petrarchan love, natural desire, the Protestant ethic and the expectations of Court life. In one poem, Astrophil rejects the mocking, cynical 'curious wits' and 'courtly nymphs' hypocritically chattering the clichés of love. In others, he even abuses Lord Rich, among 'rich fools', and says that Stella 'has no misfortune but that rich she is'. Stella is presented as the unattainable, inspiring love, but whose virtue 'bends that love to good'; however, the same poem concludes, 'But ah, Desire still cries, "Give me some food."'

That experience behind him, in around 1583 he was knighted and reconciled with the Queen (who had been annoyed by his criticism of a possible French marriage), who forgave him, rather coolly. She was still displeased when he married Frances Walsingham (1567–1633), daughter of Sir Francis, diplomat and the Queen's spymaster, and was doubtful about appointing him Governor of Flushing, under Leicester; eventually, she recalled him from a proposed expedition with Drake to the West Indies. A year later, on 22 September, he was wounded in the thigh at the Siege of Zutphen, when he famously redirected the water offered him to a dying soldier. The wound became gangrenous and he died in twenty-six days, Frances and his brother by him. Aubrey had a characteristic note about this, how 'he would not (contrary to the injunction of his physicians and surgeons) forbear his carnal knowledge of [Frances], which cost him his life; upon which occasion, there were some roguish verses made.' (They had a daughter, Elizabeth; if the story is true, he may have been anxious to secure the succession with a son.)

On Philip's death, Frances and Penelope went their different ways; it will be convenient to discuss Frances first.

In 1589-90 Frances married Essex (who also inherited Sidney's daughter and sword), who had just returned from his success at the Siege of Cadiz, described by Edmund Spenser in his *Prothalamion* as 'Great England's glory and the world's wide wonder ... faire branch of Honor, flower of Chevalrie'. Their son, also named Robert, was born in 1591, after which the couple was frequently apart, though she bore two daughters, in 1599 and 1600. He continued his former interest in the maids of honour; gossip suggested he was too openly flirtatious with 'the fair Mistress Bridges' (daughter of Lord Chandos), who was punished by the Queen with 'words and blows of anger, and she and Mistress Russell were put out of the Coffer Chamber'. This was partly because they had been seen going through the privy galleries 'to watch men at sport' – Essex, playing tennis. Ten months later it was reported that he was 'again fallen in love with his fairest B. it cannot choose but come to E. [the Queen's] ears; then he is undone, and all that depend on his favour.' (But it would take more than that to 'undo' him.)

He was soon involved in a more serious relationship with young Elizabeth Stanley (1575–1627), daughter of the unhappy marriage of Edward de Vere, Earl of Oxford, and Anne Cecil, Burghley's daughter. Burghley had originally wanted to marry his granddaughter to the young Earl of Southampton, who strung her along before, in effect, jilting her – which cost him dearly, as Burghley extorted large sums of money by way of compensation, but in January 1595 she was married to William Stanley, sixth Earl of Derby (1561–1642), in a very grand ceremony at Greenwich Palace. Despite the early birth of a daughter, the marriage did not go well, with the husband given cause for uneasiness, while Elizabeth liked the gaiety of Court life. Soon after this, Essex arrived in all his glory, and the affair quickly got under way. Burghley complained of her lack of care for her child, being looked after at Pymmes, his house. Lady Anne Bacon, mother of (later Sir) Francis Bacon, reported on Derby's distress: 'it is said, he loveth her greatly, as with grief laboureth to win her.' In December 1596, Lady Anne, unhappy at her son's friendship with Essex, wrote to Essex, warning of the consequences of 'the luste of concupiscence' and of 'infaming a noble man's wife and so near her majesty' (the Queen was her godmother), and especially of the husband's probable reaction: 'If a desperate rage, as commonly followeth, he will be revenged his provoked jealousy and most intolerable injury, even desperately.' Essex was not worried, and denied anything improper with 'the lady you mean'.

Essex gave Elizabeth a soldier's farewell before going on his Azores expedition in 1597, while she was sent away to live at her husband's house in Knowsley, Lancashire. Her behaviour, as reported by 'friends', drove Derby into a frenzy, threatening violence. His reputation was at stake – that he might be thought a 'wittol', a complacent cuckold. When he got to Greenwich, he was persuaded by Burghley to sign a declaration:

> If any one can say that I know my wife to be dishonest of her body or that I can justly prove it by my self or any one else, I challenge him to the combat of life. If any one suppose any speeches of mine to have proceeded out of that doubt, he doth me wrong.

He had to pretend that his wife was faithful, as he needed the support of Burghley and her relatives in his legal struggle over the Stanley estate with his brother's widow. Soon after Essex's return, gossip and the affair started up again, and Elizabeth's daughter died at Pymmes while her mother was at Court. In 1598, she and her husband separated; a reconciliation was attempted in 1599, and another daughter was born, but after that the couple had little to do with each other. Essex was busy elsewhere.

After Philip Sidney's death, Penelope, not quite the Stella embodiment of chaste virtue, but lumbered with Lord Rich, became for twenty years the open mistress of, and bore six children to, Sir Charles Blount, later Lord Mountjoy (1563–1606), tall, good-looking with brown curly hair, 'a sweet face and of a most neat composure'. Knighted after serving with Leicester in the Netherlands in 1587, the favours shown him by the Queen provoked the jealousy of Essex, who challenged him to a duel; after the necessary slight wound, with honour satisfied, Essex befriended him. The Penelope-Blount relationship was not kept secret. George Peele's verse *Polyhymnia* (1590), describing the jousting ceremonies at the Accession Day tilts, mentions Blount and his emblems:

> Comes Sir Charles Blount, in or and azure dight;
> Rich in his colours, richer in his thoughts,
> Rich in his fortunes, honour, arms and art.

Rich was by now a known cuckold, wittily noted in verse as 'Lord Rich, Cornu Copia' (rich and profusely horned). Mountjoy had campaigned vigorously in Ireland and was appointed Essex's successor as lord lieutenant there in October 1599, and when Essex went off there he lent his country house, Chartley, in Staffordshire to Penelope and her cousin, Elizabeth Vernon (1572–1655), recently a maid of honour but now in disgrace for having married Henry Wriothesley, Earl of Southampton, without permission, in 1598. Essex got Southampton out of prison and made him general of horse in Ireland, again without permission.

While the young women were there, Rich wanted Penelope to come to London, but she would not leave Elizabeth, who wrote to her husband for permission to go. Her letter concluded, memorably, with a PS:

> All the news I can send you that I thinke wil make you mery is that I read in a letter from London that Sir John Falstaf is by his Mistress Dame Philpot made father of a godly millers thum, a boye that's all head and very litel body; but this is a secrit.

The reference is to an enemy of Essex, Lord Cobham, a descendant of the original of Falstaff, now busy pursuing possible wives, like Falstaff in *The Merry Wives of Windsor*. It would be good to know to what event this refers.

After the debacle of the Ireland campaign and Essex's unapproved return, both women pleaded for their men. Southampton, a lesser figure, was banned from Court but passed his time in London merely going to plays every day. Essex was in more deadly trouble. Not allowed to visit him in prison, Penelope made a nuisance of herself with constant pleading and pressure. She dressed in black of the cheapest material, to denote humility and distress, pestering Court friends for help, and was at last allowed a brief visit in December 1599. Meanwhile, Essex engaged in secret communication with King James in Scotland, via letters by Penelope in code (Penelope was Rialta, the king, Victor, the queen, Venus, and Essex, the Weary Knight). She may have urged him to take more vigorous action, and even been involved, to some extent, on the day of his disastrous failed coup attempt in January 1601 (planned in Southampton's London house, but without support from Mountjoy). In the Tower, Essex shamefully accused Penelope, 'a proud spirit', of being the driving force. She was examined by Burghley and the Lord Admiral, when she said she had been 'more like a slave than a sister', and had been maligned. She was later released into Rich's custody. Essex was executed on 25 February 1601; Southampton was tried for treason but reprieved, and kept in the Tower until the accession of James, who restored his forfeited earldom.

In 1605, Rich (one is inclined to write, 'poor Rich') at last obtained a divorce of sorts (*a mensa et thoro*), which did not legally permit remarriage. Despite this, Penelope and Mountjoy, now the Earl of Devonshire, were married on St Stephen's Day, 1605, by his chaplain, William Laud, later Archbishop of Canterbury. Ever persistent, in that year Mountjoy published a defence of his marriage, describing how

> A lady, of great birth and virtue, being in the power of her friends, was by them married, against her will, unto one against whom she did protest at the very solemnity, and ever after; between whom, from the first day, there ensued continued discord, although the same fears that forced her to marry constrained her to live with him. Instead of a

comfort, he did study in all things to torment her; and by
fear and fraud did practise to deceive her of her dowry.

The criticism of Rich is not very persuasive. Part of the object of this
was to protect their children born before this dubious marriage. It was all
in vain; James was shocked, and forbade them the Court. Mountjoy died
in 1606, and Penelope the next year. She left six children by Rich – in
theory – and five by Mountjoy; that, at any rate, was the theory.

We may conclude this section with a maid of honour, a member of
the Sidney family, who escaped direct entanglement with Essex. Philip
Sidney's sister, Mary (1561–1621) had been at Court since 1575, and in
1577, aged 16, was married to Henry Herbert (c. 1538–1601), second
Earl of Pembroke and nephew of Queen Catherine Parr; at 39, it was his
third marriage. At the wedding, the Earl of Leicester advanced part of
her dowry, owing to her father's reduced resources. Despite the disparity
of their ages, the marriage went on well enough.

Aubrey said she was 'a beautiful lady and had an excellent wit, and
had the best breeding that that age could afford [she was well educated,
acquiring a knowledge of Latin, Greek and Hebrew]. She had a pretty
sharp-oval face. Her hair was of a reddish-yellow.' Aubrey thought that
her husband kept her away from Court temptations to live in Wilton
House, the Pembroke seat near Salisbury. Pembroke was happy to support
her literary and cultural interests; under her influence Wilton House
became a kind of salon for Elizabethan poets and intellectuals, including
Edmund Spenser, Samuel Daniel, John Donne and Sir John Harington.
Nicholas Breton wrote of it as 'a kind of little Court', and compared it
to Castiglione's famous court of intellectuals at Urbino. She encouraged
and published Philip's writings and completed his verse adaptations of
the Psalms, as well as producing her own writings and two sons, William
and Herbert (joint dedicatees of the Shakespeare First Folio). After her
husband's death, she remained at Wilton, encouraging the drama. In the
nineteenth century, a writer claimed to have seen a letter from her at
Wilton, apropos a visit by royalty in 1603, which said, 'We have the man
Shakespeare with us', but no-one else has seen it. Aubrey concluded his
account of her with an epitaph by William Browne:

Underneath this sable hearse
Lies the subject of all verse:

Sidney's sister, Pembroke's mother;
Death, ere thou hast slain another,
Fair, and learn'd, and good as she,
Time shall throw a dart at thee.

It is a relief to conclude with a more admirable, and perhaps happier, character than most of those in this section.

* * * * *

The Blood Royal

While some at Court were able to exploit their royal connections, for others, especially the women, it was a real misfortune. The Grey sisters – the ladies Jane, Catherine and Mary – could have told of this blight. Lady Catherine Grey (c. 1538-1568), younger sister of 'the Nine Days' Queen', Jane Grey (married at 16 in 1553, executed the next year), was herself a theoretical claimant to the throne, but annoyed the Queen by complaining at not being formally recognised as heir presumptive. It was even reported to Sir William Cecil by the English ambassador to Spain that King Philip considered stealing her out of the realm and marrying her to his son Don Carlos, or some other member of the family, and setting up her title against that of Mary Stuart. Like her sister, she was never a free woman; sexually taboo to most men as a possible spouse or mother of some other claimant.

At 15, she was espoused – possibly even married – to Henry, second Earl of Pembroke, but that was dissolved on the accession of Queen Mary (probably to his relief). In about 1560 she began a romance with the brother of Lady Jane Seymour and cousin of Edward VI, Edward Seymour (1539–1621), son of the Lord Protector, who was made Earl of Hertford in 1559. They needed the permission of the Queen, but their go-between, her mother, Frances Brandon, Duchess of Suffolk, who had notoriously married her master of horse, Adrian Stokes, sixteen years her junior, unfortunately died just when they needed her. (Edward's mother, widow of Protector Somerset, had married her steward, Francis Newdigate, so irregular marriages were not unknown there.) They decided to go ahead with a secret marriage late that November, and hope for the Queen's forgiveness later.

Accordingly, Catherine and Lady Jane dodged going on a royal hunting trip to Eltham Palace, pleading severe toothache, and made their way to Hertford's place. There, it turned out that he had not managed to arrange for a priest, but Jane succeeded in finding a Catholic priest (somehow) and paid him £10, a considerable amount, to perform the service, after which he prudently disappeared. Henry gave Catherine a five-piece ring, in which was inscribed, 'As circles five by art compact, shewe but one ring in sight, So trust uni[t]eth faithfull minds with knott of secret might. Whose force to break but greedie death no wight possesseth power, As tyme and sequel well shall prove, my ring can say no more.' Then they all went quietly back to Whitehall.

Soon Hertford was sent abroad on a diplomatic mission, while Catherine, alone (Jane Seymour died in March 1561) and now pregnant, was left behind in considerable distress and anxiety. She turned to confide in someone experienced in such matters, Lady St Loe, better known to history as 'Bess of Hardwick' (1527–1608), herself eventually married and widowed four times but at present on her third husband, Sir William St Loe. Bess – to call her that – no romantic, reproved her bitterly for her folly, and told a few people. Still looking for help, Catherine went to Robert Dudley (later Earl of Leicester in 1564), creeping nervously into his room at night. Horrified, he got her out straight away, and next morning told the Queen.

Catherine was sent to the Tower, though not in great discomfort, where she was interrogated about every detail of the ceremony, as was Hertford, who had been summoned back to the Tower. They both claimed to have forgotten the date of the ceremony, though later Catherine remembered the Eltham Palace outing (when officials settled on 27 November). The commission of inquiry obediently found that no marriage had taken place. In September 1561 she bore a son, also named Edward. She and Hertford were supposed to be kept apart, but turnkeys can turn keys, if properly oiled, and she bore a second son, Thomas, in February 1563. The marriage was declared invalid and the boys illegitimate, and Hertford fined £15,000, a huge amount, by the Star Chamber, for 'seducing a virgin of the blood royal', though much of this was remitted by the Queen. Catherine was kept in the custody of her uncle, Lord John Grey, but never saw Hertford again – did she get to keep that wedding ring? – and disappeared from view, dying in 1568, aged around 30. The Queen paid £74 for a superior funeral at Salisbury Cathedral, befitting her status.

In 1582, after a delay of fourteen years, including several in prison, Hertford married Frances Howard, sister of Admiral Howard and Lady Douglas Sheffield; again the marriage was kept secret and she was able to continue as gentlewoman of the privy chamber. In 1595, he tried to have that marriage set aside and his first marriage validated and his sons legitimised (with theoretical claims to the throne), for which he was again imprisoned. Indomitably, after the death of Lady Frances in 1598, he married yet another Frances (née Howard), a wealthy widow, and in 1602 avoided another stay in the Tower by telling the government of the attempted marriage of Ar[a]bella Stuart, a claimant to the throne, to his grandson. He kept going into his eighties, dying in 1621, when his widow provided a large, ornate tomb in Salisbury Cathedral, before promptly marrying for the third time.

The wedding bells rang for some, but not for diminutive Mary Grey, a little over 4 feet in height and 'a little, crooked back and very ugly', according to the Spanish ambassador. She fell for the 6 feet 6 inches tall Thomas Keys, serjeant porter of the Queen's Watergate in Whitehall. He may have felt sorry for the little woman, and believe that he might be raised socially after the initial furore; she had no-one else to hope for. After exchanges of glances, smiles and gifts, they got married secretly, by candle light, on 16 July 1565 in Westminster Palace by the usual unknown priest – 'old, fat and of low stature,' it was later stated. The Queen was predictably angered; Keys went to Fleet Prison for three years, Lady Mary to the care of the mother of the maids and then to the unwelcoming Duchess of Suffolk, who complained about her lack of possessions which the duchess resented having to supply. There Mary stayed until Catherine's death in 1568, before being transferred, first to the household of her stepfather, Adrian Stokes, and then to her own house, in Greenwich. Keys was released and freed to live in Lewisham, where he died in 1571, to Lady Mary's grief. She was allowed to attend Court festivals at Hampton Court in 1576, and to present small gifts to the Queen. She continued to sign herself 'Mary Keys', and died on 20 April 1578, aged about 33.

Another young woman whose life was blighted by having royal connections was Lady Ar[a]bella Stuart (1575–1615), daughter of Charles Stuart, Earl of Lennox, great-grandson of Henry VII, and brought up by her grandmother, Bess of Hardwick, who had cannily married her daughter Elizabeth Cavendish (by her second husband, Sir William Cavendish) to the Earl, who conveniently died soon after fathering Arbella. By this connection, Arbella was as close to the English throne as James VI of Scotland. The Earl died when she was only a year old, and her mother when she was 7, so she was transferred to the care of Bess and her aunt, Lady Mary Talbot (née Cavendish). Mary (1556–1632) was married at the age of 12 to Gilbert Talbot (later seventh Earl of Shrewsbury), whom she grew up to dominate. Francis Bacon once remarked, 'The Earl of Shrewsbury is a great man but there is a greater than he, which is my Lady of Shrewsbury.' Clearly very much her mother's daughter, she was intellectual and well educated – her portrait at St John's College, Cambridge shows a very strong face.

Arbella was also well educated and good-looking (even pretty, in her portrait in the National Portrait Gallery), with a fair claim to the throne. There was some talk of her being married to her cousin, James, or to the son of the Duke of Parma (a descendant of John of Gaunt), or even with Leicester's baby son, Robert, who died in 1584. She was briefly at Elizabeth's Court until a Roman Catholic plot to kidnap her was discovered, or invented, when she was sent back to Bess at Hardwick (presumably considered more secure than the Court). Ten frustrated years later, at about 27, she tried to marry – in secret, of course – another Edward Seymour, this one the elder grandson of the Earl of Hertford and so a descendant of Henry VII; grandfather shrewdly told the authorities, and that was the end of that.

Following James I's accession to the throne, she was allowed to attend Court, and life brightened for a while, but in 1609 she was put under restraint (presumably watched over in some form of house arrest) for allegedly planning to marry. On 22 June 1610, now aged 35, she actually managed to get away and marry Edward's younger brother, William Seymour (1588–1660), grandson of Lady Catherine Grey, thirteen years her junior. Within three weeks they were caught, arrested and imprisoned, William in the Tower and Arbella in Lambeth. The next year, while being transferred north to the Bishop of Durham, she stopped at Highgate and with the assistance of Lady Shrewsbury's man, 'that trusty rogue, Compton', she got away again and disguised herself as a man, in a man's doublet, a man-style peruque with long locks over her hair, a black cloak, russet boots with red tops, and a rapier by her side. She dodged the guards at Barnet, and sailed for the Netherlands to meet her husband, who had escaped from the Tower, at Ostend. However, she was overtaken at sea, and brought back to be interrogated by James's Privy Council, and then to imprisonment in the Tower, as was Lady Mary Talbot, who had helped her. Despite many appeals to the king, she was never released, and reportedly starved herself to death four years later, dying aged 40.

When Lady Mary's case was heard in the Star Chamber, in 1612, she acted with 'high and great contempt', saying the proceedings were 'but tricks and gigs', demanding as a peeress to be tried by peers or not at all, and refusing to answer, because, she said, of a vow she had taken. She was fined £20,000 and confined to the Tower until 1615, the year of her husband's death. In 1618, investigations were undertaken to discover whether Arbella had had a child, a question Mary refused to answer, which got her back into the Tower until 1623. William Seymour later lived in exile in Paris, was eventually reconciled with the king, and married Frances Devereux, daughter of the executed Earl of Essex; he himself survived to welcome the Restoration of Charles II in 1660.

Chapter 7

The Heart and Stomach of a Queen

On 9 August 1588, at Tilbury, at the coming of the dreaded Spanish Armada, Queen Elizabeth, then aged 55, claimed that, despite having 'the body of a weak and feeble woman', she had 'the heart and stomach of a king'. Pride and spirit she always had, but in so far as heart and stomach related to love and physicality, they were a trouble and frustration for her throughout her life, inseparable from her role as queen and monarch. To discuss her love life, such as it was, cannot escape some consideration of her public, political life.

Troubled Wit

Things had gone badly from the beginning: her mother, Queen Anne Boleyn, executed on the charge of incestuous adultery with her brother, was looked on as tainted stock. In (Catholic) theory, Henry VIII's first two marriages, with Catherine of Aragon and Anne Boleyn, were incestuous, supposing that Henry's older brother and heir to the throne, Prince Arthur, had slept with his wife Catherine (which she claimed and Henry denied). Consequently, both his daughters, Mary and Elizabeth, were illegitimate. As the product of an incestuous, illegitimate union, Elizabeth was viewed as 'an insatiable sexual deviant herself'.[1] One stepmother, Jane Seymour, died in childbirth, and another, Catherine Howard, was also executed for adultery when Elizabeth was 8 and a 1/2 years old – all very off-putting, possibly even traumatic, for a girl of any sensitivity. About four years later, she laboriously translated from the French, and dedicated to her next and last stepmother, Queen Katherine Parr, a dauntingly severe work, *The Mirrour or Glasse of the Synneful Soule*, a study of a subject of appreciable interest to the Tudors, the theological implications of incestuous relationships (as widely defined), how easily caught up in, and how escaped.[2]

On Henry's death in 1547, Katherine wasted no time in marrying the man she originally wanted, Sir Thomas Seymour, the good-looking, red-bearded, aggressively masculine brother of Edward Seymour, Duke of Somerset and Lord Protector; he probably thought this marriage would provide a useful connection, without taking into account that being married might cramp his style in the future. Elizabeth was kept out of the way in Chelsea, receiving a very thorough education: history, geography, Greek, Latin, French, Spanish, and Italian, with a little Welsh thrown in by her nurse, Blanche Parry (ap Harry). About twenty-five years older than Elizabeth, Blanche was officially lady-in-waiting – effectively nurse and stepmother – from the girl's earliest years. Unfortunately, Sir Thomas engaged in what would now be recognised as sexual grooming. In the mornings he would come into her bedroom to say good morning, and 'strike her upon the back or buttocks familiarly' or 'pull back the bed curtains and make as though he would come at her', as she retreated. Once he even tried to kiss her in bed, but was told to go away by her nurse and governess, Kat Ashley, who reported all this later. He would make early morning visits to her bedroom 'bare legged in only his nightshirt'.

When they moved to Hanworth in Middlesex, Katherine even joined in, as they both tickled her in bed; on one occasion he cut up her dress 'into a hundred pieces' while Katherine held her back; what larks. Perhaps Katherine felt that matters were getting out of hand – he had obtained keys to Elizabeth's apartments, and would let himself in unexpectedly – and in May 1548, herself now pregnant at 36, she sent 15-year-old Elizabeth away, to the household of Sir Anthony Denny, with Kat's sister. Here she was kept in relative seclusion – more extensive studying with the noted scholar, Roger Ascham, author of *The Scholemaster* – which led to rumours that she had been made pregnant by Seymour: a local midwife claimed to have helped a 'very fair young lady', whose child subsequently died.[3]

When Katherine died, Seymour was back at Elizabeth again, this time with Ashley's support – who knew what might come of such a marriage? Blanche's brother, Sir Thomas Parry, Elizabeth's inept treasurer, passed on the suggestion that she might consider marrying Seymour, but she put him off; he also spoke to Kat, who said she 'would wish her for his wife before all men living'. However, soon after this both Kat and Thomas Parry were removed to the Tower, in connection with enquiries into Seymour's schemes to entrap young King Edward VI into marrying his cousin, Lady Jane Grey, and himself to catch Elizabeth, at which she 'did weep tenderly'. She also wrote to the Lord Protector to rebut suggestions that she was pregnant – 'My Lord, these are shameful slanders' – but declined to answer stories of romps with Seymour, though Mistress Parry reported some of this, and Kat admitted that she had 'wished both openly and privately' that Elizabeth and Seymour would marry. In the end, Seymour was condemned for treason, and beheaded on 20 March 1549, on the order of his brother.

How much he meant to her, or that she would care to admit to, might be suggested by a remark attributed to her: 'this day died a man with much wit and very little judgement.' She pleaded for clemency for Kat Ashley: while Kat was in custody, people would think that Elizabeth was guilty of the claimed 'lewd behaviour'. Her good reputation was absolutely essential.

She had been unwell all that summer; her health was rarely strong, with irregular menstruation; many of her illnesses coincided with difficult emotional times and appear to have been at least psychosomatic in origin. Now she seemed noticeably better and more content. On 17 March, six months after her sixteenth birthday, she rode into London with a large retinue to visit her brother the King; from now on, she was more in the public eye.

With Edward's death and the accession of Mary in 1553, life became difficult for her again, regarded as she was with mistrust by the new Queen's advisers. There was pressure on her to convert to Roman Catholicism; she went to Mass in the Royal Chapel in Whitehall, complaining of severe pain, and asked one of the Queen's ladies to rub her stomach for her (later she went sufficiently regularly). There were discussions about marrying her off; various Catholics were considered, particularly Edward Courtenay, Edward IV's great-great-grandson, recently released from the Tower by Mary. Unappealing, pale, with a rather vacant expression, he was no great catch – and was not all that keen on her. Nevertheless, they were often seen together, until it was feared that, both heirs to the throne, they could become a threat, and the relationship was brought to an end. Simon Renard, Charles V's ambassador, thought it would be better to execute them both. When the Wyatt rebellion broke out in 1554, she was under suspicion and interred in the Tower for two months, before being transferred to the royal manor at Woodstock, where she wrote some verses,[4] one beginning:

> Oh, fortune, thy wresting wavering state
> Hath fraught with cares my troubled wit,
> Whose witness this present prison late
> Could bear ...

Edward Courtenay was sent into exile, and died soon afterwards.

In 1557, Queen Mary was dying, and (consequently, one might think) Elizabeth was unwell once more. On 17 November 1558 Queen Mary died, and Elizabeth automatically acceded to the throne. According to what sounds like a PR statement, when informed of this by privy councillors and Sir Nicholas Throckmorton, in the garden at Hatfield, she was sitting under an oak tree (where else, in November?), reading the Bible in Greek, and quoted from Psalm 118, 'This is the Lord's doing; it is marvellous in our eyes.'

* * * * *

Sweet Bessie and Robert

Now, in Hatfield, she made her first appointments. Sir William Cecil, 38, shrewd, capable, loyal, was to be principal secretary of state; she said that he would 'not be corrupted by any manner of gifts'; instead he made large amounts of money from his other appointments (he was created Baron Burghley in 1571). Among more immediate appointments, Kat Ashley was made first lady of the bedchamber, and her husband, John, keeper of the Queen's jewels; Blanche Parry was to be keeper of the royal books and her husband, despite his previous incompetence, treasurer of the royal household. She had a close entourage of ladies: four ladies of the bedchamber, three more as chamberers, seven in the privy chamber, and a gaggle of maids of honour.

Elizabeth herself, now 25, was about 5 feet 4 inches tall, slim, with her father's red-gold hair and her mother's black eyes, a long oval face, thin lips and a pale complexion. Fashion demanded white skin, fair hair and a high, smooth forehead, which she had by nature. Others had to bleach their hair somehow; there is no record of their adopting the Venetian ladies' method of rinsing in urine. She washed her hands with meticulous care; adjoining her bedroom was an elaborate bath, where, a noble foreign visitor observed, 'the water pours from oyster shells and different kinds of rock.' (Elizabethans generally bathed infrequently, believing this to be unhealthy, but washed regularly, sprinkling their bodies liberally with scent.) As for skin-whitening, this was generally achieved with a powder of ground alabaster; Elizabeth also use egg white, powdered eggshell, alum and borax. White lead mixed with vinegar and mercury sublimate might be used in powder form, with long-term disastrous effects. As Richard Haydocke reported, 'which way soever it be used, it is very offensive to man's flesh'.[5] For rouge and lip salve, ceruse, with lead hydroxide, madder, red ochre and red crystalline mercuric sulphide and cochineal were used. In effect, Elizabeth and her ladies were coating their faces with poison. She soon started losing her hair, probably from these various treatments, so her apothecary made up a special pomade, and she changed her hairstyle. As Ben Jonson asked, in *Sejanus* (1603):

> What lady sleeps with her own face a'nights?
> Which puts her teeth off, with her own clothes, in court?
> Or which her hair? Which her complexion?
> And in which box she puts it?

As she aged, her addiction to sugars and sweets (an addiction common to most ladies at the time) rotted and discoloured her teeth, so that she had to counter her bad breath with mouthwashes. She did not cope well with toothache; once, when a tooth was giving her great pain, some of her councillors urged her to have it out. She refused, until the Bishop of London volunteered to have one of his pulled out, to show how easy and (relatively) painless this might be. Despite this heroic self-sacrifice, she was not persuaded, and spent many of her latter days with her finger in her mouth, perhaps rubbing the tooth with rosemary or expensive cloves. But all that was in the years to come; now, she was youthful, lively and attractive.

Soon after she became Queen, her first professed lover appeared, in William Birch's welcoming *A Songe between the Quenes majestie and*

Englande (1558).[6] It is the first to raise the suggestion that she is to be married to England, an idea she was to develop later:

> E: Come over the born bessy,
> > Come over the born bessy,
> > > Swete bessy come over to me
> > And I shall thee take,
> > and my dere lady make
> > > Before all other that ever I see.
> B: My thinke I hear a voice,
> > at whome I do rejoice,
> > > and aunswer the now I shall
> > Tel me I say,
> > what art thou that biddes me come away
> > > and so earnestly doost me call.
> E: I am thy lover faire,
> > hath chose the to mine heir
> > > and my name is mery Englande
> > Therefore come away,
> > and make no more delaye
> > > Swete bessie give me thy hande.
> B: Here is my hand,
> > My dere lover Englande
> > > I am thine both with mind and hart
> > For ever to endure,
> > thou maiest be sure
> > > Untill death us two depart …

(Interestingly, Shakespeare quotes from this in *King Lear*.)

As a young, single queen, Elizabeth had several other, more serious suitors: Erik XIV of Sweden, Charles, Archduke of Austria (nephew of Philip II); the earls of Arran and Arundel brought up the rear. More significant among those appointed to her Privy Council was a tall, handsome young man, one year older than herself, Lord Robert Dudley, fifth son of the Duke of Northumberland and fortunate survivor of Mary's reign, and now Elizabeth's master of horse.

She was clearly attracted to him, and lavished preferments on him, creating him Knight of the Garter and Constable of Windsor Castle, with extensive lands at Kew and in Yorkshire, and licence to export woollen cloth duty free, and more. He was a fine horseman, energetic, interested in drama and dancing, especially the lavolta and galliard that she enjoyed dancing with him, with its leap in the air. There was, however, one drawback: he was married, since 1550, to Amy Robsart of Norfolk.

Despite that, the flirtation and serious mutual attraction, and Dudley's pursuit, were obvious and widely commented upon. The Spanish ambassador reported in 1559:

> During the last four days Lord Robert has come so much into favour that he does what he likes with affairs and it is even said that her Majesty visits him in his chamber day and night. People talk of this so freely that they go so far as to say that his wife has a malady in one of her breasts and that the Queen is only waiting for her to die so she can marry her Robert.[7]

One night, when riding back from Dudley's house at Kew, she chatted to the torchbearers about his admirable qualities and the further honours she might grant him. One of them passed this on, and it reached Cecil, who was very worried. He mentioned his concern to the ambassador, who reported, 'he perceives the most manifest ruin impending over the Queen through her intimacy with Lord Robert. Lord Robert has made himself master of the business of the State and of the person of the Queen, to the extreme misery of the realm, with the purpose of marrying her,' adding that Dudley led her 'to spend all day hunting with much danger to her life and health.'

Cecil was not the only one worried. In August 1559, Kat Ashley went so far as to kneel before the Queen and beg her to put an end to the 'disreputable rumours' regarding her relationship with Dudley, but Elizabeth insisted that there was 'no just cause' for them. Nevertheless, the rumours were widespread among ordinary people. In 1560, Anne Down of Brentford was jailed for spreading a story that Elizabeth had had two children by Lord Robert. When the man she told, said, 'Why, she hath no child yet', Down replied, 'He hath put one to the making.' In

1563, Edmund Baxter said her unchastity disqualified her as a monarch: 'Lord Robert kept her Majesty, and that she was a naughty woman and could not rule her realm.' His wife added, that when she had seen the Queen at Ipswich, 'she looked like one lately come out of childbed.' Later, Henry Hawkins explained her frequent progresses throughout the country as a way to get away from observation at Court and have her children by Dudley: 'She never goeth in progress but to be delivered.'[8]

Then, in September 1560, it was reported that Amy Robsart's servants, returned from a day at Abingdon Fair, found her dead, lying at the foot of the stairs with her neck broken. There were local suspicious mutterings. Dudley, who had been at Court, immediately instituted an inquiry, which came in with a verdict of accidental death; he arranged for a funeral at St Mary the Virgin Church in Oxford, but did not attend nor order a monument. For a while he stayed away from Court, but soon the flirtation was open once more. In November 1561, Elizabeth disguised herself as a maid of Katherine Knollys's niece in order to watch him shooting at Windsor and, later that month, she secretly dined at his house. One day, during a boating trip on the Thames, after some extremely bold flirting on his part, he went so far as to propose that Alvaro de la Quadra, one of the party, who was a bishop as well as a diplomat, might as well marry them right there, which the Queen put off by suggesting that the bishop's English might not be sufficient for the ceremony. Shortly after this, the scandal of the marriage between Lady Catherine Grey and Edward Seymour broke. Partly in reaction, Elizabeth was ill, described as 'dropsical ... falling away and is extremely thin and the colour of a corpse'. In the same year, Mary Stuart went to Scotland, when Elizabeth suggested to one of Mary's advisers that she was her preferred successor.

After a progress through East Anglia (when presumably Mistress Baxter saw her at Ipswich), she returned to London, but by October 1562 she was feeling unwell again. A German physician, Dr Burcot, was sent for, who immediately diagnosed smallpox, the deadly disease of the time. The symptoms of this 'common and familiar disease' were well known, according to one contemporary. As they developed, worryingly, the council discussed the possibility of arranging her succession, some speaking for Lady Catherine Grey, some for Mary Stuart; Dudley for Henry Hastings, Earl of Huntingdon, coincidentally married to his sister. In her distressed state, Elizabeth asked them to appoint Dudley as Lord Protector, at the exorbitant rate of £20,000 a year. She also asked that his groom of the chamber, Tamworth, who slept in his room, should receive £500 a year. Noticing their reaction, she swore that, although she loved Sir Robert, there had been nothing wrong in their relationship; some people wondered whether Tamworth was receiving hush money.

She had previously dismissed Dr Burcot, who was made to come back, rather against his offended amour-propre. He immediately prescribed a traditional treatment, of wrapping her in a length of scarlet cloth, laying her in front of a fire, and giving her some potion. When red spots appeared on her hand, she asked what they indicated. ''Tis the pox,' he replied irritably, 'God's pestilence! Which is better? To have the pox in the hand or in the face, or in the heart and kill the whole body?' Elizabeth recovered, with relatively little facial scarring, but Mary Sidney, Dudley's sister, who had nursed her throughout the illness, was very severely scarred. Her husband, Sir Henry, later wrote, 'I left her a full fair lady, in mine eyes at least the fairest, and when I returned [from Ireland] I found her as foul a lady as the smallpox could make her, which she did take by continued attendance upon her Majesty's most precious person.' The Queen rewarded Burcot with lands and a pair of golden spurs (very useful for a doctor), but wishing 'never to be reminded of her illness', expressed no great sympathy or gratitude to Lady Mary, who withdrew from the Court and public life.

The Queen herself returned to active Court life and business, retreating to Windsor Castle in 1563 to avoid the outbreak of plague brought back from Europe by English soldiers – about a thousand died in one week. She was not, as she said herself, 'a morning woman'; her morning toilet, assisted by her ladies, was a long-drawn-out affair, with many cosmetics to apply, and layers of clothes to choose: linen underwear (knickers were not usual at the time), a flat-fronted bodice, kept flat by rigid busks and pointed to below the waist, with a farthingale skirt with its many pinnings and underskirt, a brightly coloured dress in yellow or red, often with silver embroidery, knitted silk stockings (once she had been given a pair, she never wore woollen stockings again), slippers of cloth of silver, and ropes of pearls from the West Indies. She had very many clothes to choose from, not only what she had chosen for herself, but what had been given her by courtiers or foreign diplomats. An inventory made towards the end of her life included 102 'french gownes', 100 'loose gownes', sixty-seven 'round gownes', with ninety-nine robes, 127 cloaks, eighty-five doublets, 125 petticoats, fifty-six outer skirts, 126 kirtles, eighteen mantles and

136 'foreparts' (stomachers).[9] After a light breakfast, prayers and a brisk walk in the garden, she would get down to work, with papers or meetings. She ate little; dining was a laboriously ceremonial affair, state banquets even more so. In the evenings there might be a masque or play, or dancing and music. In her own chamber, she might amuse herself with playing cards or 'tables' (a kind of backgammon). Perhaps surprisingly, she enjoyed bear-baiting, and had her own team of bears and mastiffs.

On 29 September 1564, she appointed Robert Dudley as Earl of Leicester (at the ceremony, a courtier noticed, she put her hand down his neck, and tickled him as she fastened the mantle on his shoulders). This was done partly in consequence of the discussion that he should marry Mary Stuart (herself not long recovered from smallpox), who would not consider marrying someone who was not a noble. He himself was unwilling, whilst Mary had her eye on another man, a handsome Roman Catholic, twelve years younger than Leicester, Henry Stewart, Lord Darnley. As negotiations dragged on, with flattering accounts of Darnley ('the lustiest and best proportioned long man' that Mary had seen), Elizabeth was unwell again – gastric influenza, probably. The Scots ambassador, Sir James Melville, thought that Elizabeth was too keen on Leicester to approve the marriage. On one occasion, she took Melville into her privy chamber to show him some of her miniatures, kept in a cabinet there; each was wrapped in paper, with a name written on it. One was marked, 'My Lord's picture'; when Melville asked to see the contents, it was a portrait of Leicester. He asked if he might take it to show Mary, but Elizabeth would not let it go.

The intimacy between Elizabeth and Leicester continued openly. After a game of tennis, Leicester had even taken a napkin out of the Queen's hand, and wiped his face with it. They were seen kissing on an open highway in London, and driving in the Queen's coach to Greenwich Palace, where he was reported to have been seen in her bedchamber. He himself expressed little real hope of their marriage. One day, he told the French ambassador that the Queen had said that if she were ever to marry an English man, he would be her choice, but she always insisted she would never marry.

To the latest Spanish ambassador, Guzman de Silva, she complained,[10]

> The world thinks a woman cannot live unmarried, and if
> she refrains from men that she does so for some bad reason,

as they used to say of me that I avoided doing so because I was fond of the Earl of Leicester whom I could not marry because he had a wife living. His wife is now dead and yet I do not marry him, although I have been pressed to do so, even by your king.

She went on:

They charge me with a great many things in my own country and elsewhere, and amongst others, that I show more favour to Robert than is fitting, speaking of me as they might of an immodest woman. I am not surprised that the occasion of it should have been given by a young woman and a young man of good qualities, to whose merits I have shown favour, although not so much as he deserves, but God knows how great a slander it is.

Intriguingly, she asked Guzman about Philip II's widowed sister, and Guzman reported her as saying 'how much she would like to see her, and how well so young a widow and a maiden would get on together, and what a pleasant life they could lead. She (the Queen) being the elder would be the husband and her Highness the wife.'[11] She would want to preserve her superior status in any relationship, and meanwhile, in her little fantasy, would welcome an escape from her male suitors and their probable demands. As a female monarch, Elizabeth had usurped the male role, and was well-nigh a king; her anomalous position in a patriarchal, hierarchical society was psychologically unsettling for everyone.

In July 1565, to Elizabeth's grief, Kat Ashley, the nearest she had had to a mother, died. Blanche Parry, her longest-serving lady, was now chief gentlewoman of the privy chamber; people said that the Court was now 'under the rule of Mistress Blanche Parry'. In the same month, Mary Stuart married her Lord Darnley, seriously damaging her relationship with the Queen of England. That winter, Lettice Knollys arrived in Court; her pregnancy did not prevent Leicester from wooing her, further provoking Elizabeth's jealousy. At the same time, the French ambassador told Guzman that Elizabeth had slept with Leicester in her chamber at Whitehall on New Year's Eve, but the Spaniard, suspecting diplomatic game-playing, doubted this.

Meanwhile, efforts to marry her off continued. Cecil tried once more for the Archduke Charles, and Catherine de Medici counter-offered her son, Charles IX, King of France, in his middle teens. Elizabeth told the French ambassador that his king was 'both too big and too small': France was too big, and the king only a boy. The ambassador still went ahead with discreet enquiries as to whether Elizabeth could have a child. One of her physicians reportedly replied, 'Your King is seventeen and the Queen is no more than thirty-two. Take no notice of what she says on the subject. If the King marries her, I will undertake that she could have ten children, and no-one knows her condition better than I do.'

In 1566, Leicester asked permission to leave the Court, ostensibly to visit his sister, Catherine, Lady Huntingdon, who was unwell; by March, Elizabeth herself was unwell and very thin, and he was asked to return, for her sake. News came of trouble in Mary Stuart's marriage with her vicious, drunken husband, Darnley (or King Henry, as the Scots were encouraged to call him). When she became pregnant, Darnley was persuaded to believe that her French confidential secretary, David Riccio, was the father, and had him murdered. He then persuaded Mary to join him in hunting down the actual murderers and driving them across the border into England. Elizabeth was shocked and outraged, but would not grant Mary's request to have them extradited from England. In May, she was ill of a fever, and wanted Leicester to return, which, with some unwillingness, he at last did. Now came news of Mary, ten years younger than Elizabeth, having given birth to a son, James, so providing the Scots with an heir. Elizabeth lamented to her ladies, 'The Queen of Scots is lighter of a fair son, while I am but a barren stock.' Once again, she was harried with demands that she marry and secure the succession.

On 3 November, a delegation of thirty Members of Parliament approached her at Whitehall, where they received a forceful reply, to the effect that they were on the verge of committing treason, and that in a monarchy it was not for the feet to tell the head what to do. She hoped to marry and have children by her husband. She said:

> As for my own part, I care not for death, for all men are
> mortal. And though I be a woman, yet I have as good a
> courage, answerable to my place, as ever my father had.
> I am your anointed Queen ... . I will never break the word
> of a Prince, spoken in public place, for my honour's sake.

> And therefore I say again, I will marry as soon as I can
> conveniently, if God take not away him with whom I mind
> to marry, or myself, or else some other great let happen.[12]

In 1567, Queen Mary fell in love with her Lord High Admiral, the Earl of Bothwell; Darnley fell ill, and she persuaded him to return to Edinburgh, when, early in the morning of 10 February his house was blown up, and his body, apparently strangled, was found 40 feet away. Mary was fairly obviously involved, to some degree; Bothwell, put on trial at his own request, was of course acquitted. He then carried her off to Dunbar Castle, where, she claimed, he raped her, before they were married by a Protestant bishop. All this effectively finished what was left of her reputation. Mary was forced to abdicate, and her young son, James, was crowned James VI. Elizabeth was outraged, and wanted to send troops to Scotland, but was distracted by war in France. Mary had been held prisoner, but, her hair cut off as a sort of disguise, escaped to Carlisle. In October she had to submit to an inquiry in York, which effectively revealed her guilt in the murder of Darnley, after which she was transferred to Bolton Castle in Yorkshire and then to Tutbury Castle in Staffordshire.

Mary's sympathisers now approached the Earl of Westmorland, the Catholic seventh Earl of Northumberland and, most importantly, the Duke of Norfolk, England's premier duke, as a possible husband. At 34, he had been married three times, his third wife having died only that year, and was well disposed to this extraordinary proposition. Elizabeth was not consulted, but somehow got wind of this scheme. Leicester was at first in favour of this, but then changed his mind. He sent a message to Elizabeth, saying he was very ill and pleaded with her to visit him; she came immediately and was told about the project; she was furious with Norfolk and demanded that he break off with Mary's advisers at once. Meanwhile, there was a crisis with Spain, after five Spanish ships were, in effect, captured and looted, and the Spanish planned reprisals, including possibly helping Westmorland and Norfolk in the north. The rebels then led an armed force south, towards Tutbury, only to find that Mary had been whisked away to Coventry; disheartened by their lack of popular support, and news of Elizabeth's forces marching against them, the so-called Rebellion of the Northern Earls fizzled out. Westmorland fled abroad, Northumberland was beheaded in York, Norfolk was sent to the Tower, and some 800 of their poorer followers were hanged. Mary, 'the daughter of debate that discord aye doth sow' (as Elizabeth wrote), had to submit to Elizabeth's terms, renouncing her claim to the English throne.

Next year, on 25 February, Pope Pius V issued a Bull of Excommunication on Elizabeth, declaring that she was an usurper, deserving of no allegiance, and that to kill her would not be a sin. A Catholic, John Felton, nailed this to the gate of the Bishop of London's palace, and was promptly found guilty of treason, hanged, disembowelled and quartered. An Italian Catholic, Roberto Ridolfi, planned to free Mary, put her on the throne of England and restore Roman Catholicism. This was to be done with the assistance of Mary's agent, the Bishop of Ross, and of Norfolk, recently released from the Tower after personally affirming his loyalty to the Queen. Cecil's agents soon got wind of this, with the help of their torturers: Ross confessed and was allowed to leave for France; Norfolk was tried and sentenced to death. After some delay and characteristic illness and stomach trouble, Elizabeth approved his execution, which at last took place on Tower Hill on 2 June 1572.

* * * * *

The Monkey and the Frog

Meanwhile, the French continued to pursue their hopes of a marriage. In 1571, Elizabeth had told the French ambassador, Bertrand Fénélon, that she would like to marry, not for herself but for the satisfaction of her subjects. Fénélon suggested Henri, Duke of Anjou: eighteen years younger than her, painted, scented, probably homosexual, he was not an attractive proposition. The French demands – that he should be joint ruler, with an income of £60,000, and allowed to attend Mass in England, in public – were impossible. In 1572 they tried again, this time offering François, Duke of Alençon, later Duke of Anjou, not yet 19, short and ugly, scarred by smallpox and with a huge nose, but intelligent, lively and not excessively Catholic. In the midst of negotiations, on St Bartholomew's Day, 24 August 1572, there was a horrific massacre of Huguenots in Paris, which set matters back. After this, another envoy, Jean de Simier, a polished courtier, witty and charming, arrived to represent his master's interests. Showing he meant business, soon after his arrival he consulted doctors as to Elizabeth's ability to bear children; reassured on this point, he made her lively addresses, even daring to creep into her bedchamber to steal a handkerchief and a nightcap to send to the duke. She was quite taken with her 'Monkey', as she called him; it was said that very early one morning she had got into his bedroom and told him to talk to her 'with only his jerkin on'. Predictably, Queen Mary repeated gossip that Elizabeth had slept with him, and other stories of Elizabeth's sexual depravity started up again. During investigations into the Ridolfi plot, one man complained that Elizabeth ignored deserving courtiers in favour of 'daunsers' who had 'more recourse to her Majesty in her Privy Chamber than reason would suffer if she were so virtuous and well inclined as some noise her.'[13] Under interrogation, Kenelm Berney asserted, 'The Queen desireth nothing but to feed her lewd fantasy, and to cut off such of her nobility as were not perfumed and court-like, to please her delicate eye and places such as were for her turn, meaning dancers, and meaning Lord Leicester and Master Hatton.'[14] Saying such things was not going to do him any good.

Elizabeth encouraged and enjoyed her courtiers' flattery and expressions of adoration, without taking them very seriously, and as ritual and applications for grants and promotion. Some years later, in 1589, she said, 'My Lord of Essex has written me some very dutiful letters, and I have been moved by them. But what I took for abundance of heart, I find to be only a suit for the farm of sweet wines' (an extremely valuable tax monopoly). Of her favourites, perhaps one of the longest-lasting, apart from Leicester, was Sir Christopher Hatton (1540–91). Tall, dark, handsome, seven years younger, a fine dancer, he specialised in particularly fulsome expressions of devotion, but rose only slowly at Court, before getting an annuity and eventual promotion to captain of her bodyguard and the vice-chamberlain of her household. He was knighted in 1577 and made a privy councillor in 1578. In 1580, in the context of the Duke of Anjou's courtship, and an outbreak of smallpox, he wrote in a letter, 'I love her no less than he that by the greatness of a kingly birth and fortune is deemed most fit to have her.' He sent her a ring for her to wear for her health, 'which hath the virtue to expel infectious airs, and is, as is telled to me, to wearen betwixt the sweet dugs – the chaste nest of more pure constancy.'

He seemed quite besotted, to a worrying degree. When he was away, ill, he wrote to her:

> No death, no, not hell, not fear of death shall ever win of me my consent so far to wrong myself again as to be absent from you one day ... . Would God I were with you but for one hour. My wits are overwrought with thoughts. I find myself amazed. Bear with me, my most dear sweet Lady. Passion overcometh me. I can write no more. Love me; for I love you.

Of course, he might have been worried about his rivals, especially Raleigh, whose favourable treatment greatly distressed him. He went so far as to send Elizabeth a bucket, with a note complaining of being 'destroyed by water' (her nickname for Sir Walter); she returned him a dove (for peace). He then sent her a jewelled bodkin, as an emblem of suicide for love, and she gave him a jewelled rainbow (no more floods). She responded to his unrelenting campaign of committed, amorously expressed devotion with the Order of the Garter, lands and estates (in 1576, she forced the Bishop of Ely to hand over his Holborn home to him – hence Hatton Gardens), used him as her spokesman in Parliament, and made him Chancellor of Oxford University and Lord Chancellor. She also made it clear that he was not expected to marry, which he never did, contenting himself with discreet mistresses.

He was briefly out of favour because of his opposition to her encouragement of the Duke of Alençon, when he told her, with tears in his eyes, that however much her people loved her, they would not forgive such a marriage, while Leicester also opposed it, though keeping quiet about his own marriage. When the French envoy, Simier, realised the extent of Leicester's opposition, he saw to it that Elizabeth should now learn of Leicester's marriage to Lettice in 1578. The Queen was furious: she demanded Leicester's immediate arrest and threatened him with the Tower of London, before settling for a lesser confinement in Greenwich Park, while Lettice was banished from Court. Eventually the Earl of Sussex managed to soothe her; Leicester gave it out that he was very ill, which brought her to his bedside, and after two days they were reconciled.

The Duke of Anjou himself now arrived, on 16 August 1579, to receive lavish Court entertainment. Elizabeth was very taken with him (perhaps on the rebound), in spite of the advertised ugliness, and enjoyed his company, calling him her 'Frog'. When he had to go back to France, he sent her messages assuring her of his love. For all this, the prospect of a French marriage aroused fierce popular opposition. In the month that he left, there appeared a pamphlet, *The Discoverie of a gaping gulf wherein England is like to be swallowed by another French marriage*, by John Stubbes, a Puritan lawyer. It warned that she was being 'led blindfold as a poor lamb to the slaughter', that she would be ruled by her young French husband, and that she was unlikely to give birth 'at these years'. The reference to her age and the suggestion that she was past childbearing were particularly hurtful. A royal proclamation banned further distribution of the pamphlet (too late, of course), Stubbes, the printer and the publisher were found guilty of publishing seditious libels, and although Elizabeth thought that Stubbes ought to be hanged, he and the printer only had their right hands chopped off. Stubbes was sent back to the Tower, where he remained for eighteen months.

In January 1580, Pope Gregory XIII re-issued the excommunication fatwa against Elizabeth, but the French persisted (full marks for effort), and in June 1581 a huge embassy was sent to negotiate with the Privy Council, and was spectacularly entertained, with great receptions at Whitehall and feasts. The Queen herself accompanied one of the embassy to see Drake's *Golden Hind* at Deptford, recently returned from its voyage around the world. As they crossed the gangplank, one of her garters came undone and slipped below the hem of her dress; the Frenchman cheekily asked if he might keep it to send to the Duke. She replied that she needed it at the time, and replaced it on her stocking, so allowing him a glimpse of her leg as she did so (*honi soit qui mal y pense*, one might say). She later gave him the garter for the Duke.

Negotiations trailed on, as usual. Several councillors wrote her a letter of opposition; Protestant Philip Sidney wrote her a letter objecting to 'a Frenchman and a Papist', which did him no good at all. For all that, when Anjou himself came over in November, she was very encouraging to him. The Spanish ambassador reported that she was 'together with the Duke in the Chamber from morning till noon, and afterwards till two or three hours after sunset. I cannot tell what the devil they do.' She persuaded Anjou to accompany her to St Paul's Cathedral, and there she kissed him in the sight of the congregation; on Accession Day (17 November), walking with him in the gallery at Whitehall, she again kissed him, on the mouth. Seeing this, the French ambassador asked if they were to be married; she took a ring from her hand and put it on the Duke's finger, and told the ambassador, 'You may tell his Majesty that the prince will be my husband.' Shortly afterwards, the Spanish ambassador reported that she summoned the ladies and gentlemen from the presence chamber into the gallery and repeated what she had just said.

Soon the whole Court knew of this, and were horrified; the privy councillors and her favourites all pleaded with her. After a sleepless night, she sent a message to the duke, that she dared not marry him without the support of her people. International and national politics prevented it: in the negotiations, the English had made impossible demands that the French could not accept (as surely she knew). The council was prepared to offer the duke £200,000 by way of compensation, but the Queen would not countenance giving up so much money. Apparently, she said that if the duke was prepared to take that instead of her, she would not marry him nor give him the money either. (It sounds like familiar espousal disputes over money.) The French now said that if she insisted on her terms, then they would have to enter into an alliance with the Spanish. Confronted with this ultimatum, Elizabeth fell ill, and then suggested that she might have to marry Anjou after all. Eventually it all collapsed: no marriage, and she (England) would pay £60,000, and, in February 1582, Anjou left. At some time, she wrote a poem, with conventional Petrarchan paradoxes, *On Monsieur's Departure*:[15]

> I grieve, and dare not show my discontent,
> I love, and yet am forced to seem to hate,
> I dote, yet dare not say I ever meant,
> I seem stark mute, yet inwardly do prate.
> > I am and am not, I freeze and yet am burned,
> > Since from my self my other self I turned.
> My care is like my shadow in the sun,
> Follows me flying, flies when I pursue it,
> Stands and lies by me, doth what I have done,
> His too familiar care doth make me rue it.
> > No means I find to rid him from my breast,
> > Till by the end of things it be suppressed.
> Some gentler passion slide into my mind,
> For I am soft and made of melting snow;

Or be more cruel, Love, and be so kind,
Let me float or sink, be high or low.
   Or let me live with some more sweet content,
   Or die and so forget what love e'er meant.

This is no spontaneous overflow, but a careful composition according to poetic conventions; what the originating feeling was, is not as obvious as it may seem.

There were those who were not surprised at what happened, believing that all her public displays of affection were as far as she could go, and part of the negotiations for a match that the Protestant group at Court would never have permitted, and that would have put the country – and her – under another's control. Whatever the truth of that, this had been her last chance of marriage – if she had really wanted it; but she could never bring herself to that, to give herself sexually and be subordinate in any sense. As it was, Anjou himself died of a fever in 1584.

Now she was about 50; portraits of the Virgin Queen were increasingly detached from physical reality: the white mask of lead, alabaster and egg white glazed over wrinkles and smallpox scars; the lead ate into her skin; her teeth were decaying and the mercuric sulphide on her lips led to some degree of mercury poisoning. Catholic assassination plots continued remorselessly: the Throckmorton Plot of 1583-4 ('more than two hundred men of all ages who, at the instigation of the Jesuits conspire to kill me,' she noted, sadly); the Babington Plot of 1585-6, a group of young Catholic gentlemen, aroused her venomous fury, as she demanded particularly cruel punishments. One young man, Chidiock Tichborne, aged 28, penned a pathetic little poem three days before his execution in 1586. In it,[16] he wrote:

My youth is gone, and yet I am but young;
I saw the world, and yet I was not seen;
My thread is cut, and yet it was not spun;
And now I live, and now my life is done … .

The complete poem was frequently copied.

It was proved that Mary Stuart was complicit in the plotting; she was tried and found guilty on 15 October; in December, after much hesitation by Elizabeth, a warrant for her execution was drawn up, and after even more hesitation, evasion and ambiguous phrasing, Elizabeth signed the warrant. William Davison, assistant to Sir Francis Walsingham, and Sir Christopher Hatton approached Lord Burghley, who, with the Privy Council, decided that the warrant should be sent to Fotheringhay Castle, where Mary was being held. On 8 February 1587, Mary, Queen of Scots was beheaded. Elizabeth was told at Greenwich Palace and showed no apparent emotion, but later experienced violent grief and anger. Davison was sent to the Tower, and Burghley was banished from the Queen's presence.

The next year saw the Spanish Armada, when she made her famous rallying speech to the troops at Tilbury; here, she promised them 'rewards and crowns ... on the word of a prince'. While she was there, word came that the armada had been overcome and scattered. The soldiers were discharged immediately the danger was over, and did not receive what they had been promised; nationally, there was joy and celebration. On Sunday, 24 November, the Queen went in procession to a thanksgiving service at St Paul's, drawn in a chariot by two white horses, like a Roman triumph.

As captain general, her old beloved, Leicester, had not done especially well, probably because of ill health. In August, he set off for Buxton, to take the waters there; on the way, he wrote to her, asking about her health: 'For my own poor case, I continue still your medicine and it amends much better than any other thing that hath been given me ... . I humbly kiss your foot.' On the way at his house in Cornbury, Oxfordshire, he developed a fever, and died there on 4 September 1588, aged 56. Before the end of the year, his widow, Lettice, married Sir Christopher Blount (not brother to Charles Blount). As at Elsinore, 'the funeral baked meats did coldly furnish forth the marriage table.' Elizabeth no doubt grieved, and gave orders for the seizure of Kenilworth Castle and his estate in Warwickshire. Perhaps she had in mind another Robert, the second Earl of Essex and now stepson of Sir Christopher.

* * * * *

The Other Robert

Leicester's place at Court and in the Queen's favour had by now been taken by Robert, Earl of Essex. Good-looking, self-confident, egotistical, ambitious, hot-headed, he was just what Elizabeth – like a lot of younger

Court ladies – fancied. People out in the country had not been keeping up with developments, and were still trotting out absurd stories about Elizabeth and Leicester: in 1589, an Essex labourer was saying that she had had two children by Leicester, and in 1590, Dionysia Deryck said that she 'hath already as many children as I, and that two of them were yet alive … and the others were burned'; another said that Leicester had 'four children by the Queen's Majesty'.[17] Obviously stupid, they were merely sentenced to the pillory.

The relationship with Essex was stormy from the start, as a result of his arrogance, bad temper and jealousy of other men she favoured. 'By God's death,' she said, 'it were fitting some one should take him down and teach him better manners, or there were no rule with him.' Her words were to prove prophetic.

He was disobedient, going off to the expedition to the Netherlands, in 1586, and only coming back, sulkily, when directly ordered. In the 1589-90 winter, he married Sidney's widow. In 1594, he claimed to have discovered a conspiracy in which Elizabeth's doctor, Roderigo Lopez (who had previously treated him for syphilis), was supposed to have tried to poison her. After prolonged torture, Lopez, almost certainly innocent, confessed, and after three months' prevarication by the Queen, was hanged, drawn and quartered.[18]

In 1598, Essex took part in a raid on Cadiz, but Elizabeth was not pleased when she did not get as much booty from this as she thought was her due. His arrogance and aggressive self-conceit began to go too far. When, in 1598, the Queen rejected his proposal that Sir George Carew be given a command in Ireland, he lost his temper and, in an insolent gesture, turned his back on her. The Queen, furious, jumped up and hit him on the side of his head, and told him, 'go and be hanged'. His hand went to his sword and he seemed about to draw, but the Earl of Nottingham intervened. Essex rushed out, saying he would never have submitted to such treatment even from King Henry VIII (a likely story!). His eventual letter of apology was no apology: 'I was never proud till your Majesty sought to make me too base … . Your Majesty by the terrible wrong you have done both me and your self, not only broke all laws of affection but done against the honour of your sex.' It is amazing that he got away with this, but there was something of a reconciliation later that year.

Things went from apparently better to bad to worse. In 1599, he was sent to Ireland to put down the rebellion led by the Earl of Tyrone,

Hugh O'Neill. His triumphant return was expected, as by the Chorus in *Henry V*, anticipating how

> Were now the general of our gracious Empress –
> As in good time he may – from Ireland coming,
> Bringing rebellion broached on his sword,
> How many would the peaceful city quit
> To welcome him …

He himself expected success and popular support. But it was not to be. He failed, disastrously, ignominiously.

In September, he decided to dash back to England, against explicit instructions, to make his case to the Queen. When he got back, the Queen was at Nonsuch Palace, in her privy chamber, not yet up and properly dressed, her grey hair loose about her face, without her wig; Essex burst in, unannounced, 'she not being ready, and he so full of dirt and mire, that his very face was full of it,' as a courtier, Rowland Whyte, reported. The shock, to Elizabeth and her women attendants, must have been almost overwhelming. No man had ever entered her bedchamber in her presence: it was sacrosanct. This was, in effect, an indecent assault, almost a rape.

Now, if ever, Elizabeth was to show the heart and stomach of a king. She could not know why Essex had come as he had, whether he had his soldiers outside, or killed any of his Court enemies, or whether she herself was in any danger. As it was, he played the loving courtier, kneeling and kissing her hands. Coolly, she listened to what he had to say, and told him to come back after he had cleaned himself up. He thought the encounter had gone well. By the time he returned, Elizabeth had been informed of the situation, that he had come with only a handful of men and that there was no immediate danger. Now he 'found her much changed in that small time, for she began to question for his return and was not satisfied in the manner of his coming away and leaving things at so great a hazard.' She dismissed him from her presence; they were never to meet again.

In October she dismissed him from all his offices; he was to remain in the house of his uncle, Sir William Knollys, until released, though forbidden to return to Court. The Queen had had enough of him. He in turn gathered his allies or acolytes, and planned an uprising, to seize control of London, the Court and the Queen. Some of his friends went to the Globe Theatre, to pay forty shillings for Shakespeare's company to perform their play, *Richard II*, featuring the deposition of a king. As Elizabeth remarked later, 'I am Richard the Second, know ye not that?' On 7 February 1601, Essex and his supporters made their move in London, but the people would not follow him, and it soon became apparent that the coup had collapsed. A royal proclamation declared that Essex was a traitor; he and his people were themselves seized and taken to the Tower. On 19 February they were tried in Westminster Hall and found guilty. Sentence of death was passed on Essex that evening. Southampton was pardoned. After her usual hesitation, Elizabeth signed the death warrant, and Essex was beheaded in the Tower six days later. The Queen was playing the virginals when she was informed. She received the news in silence. Then, after a pause, she resumed playing.

* * * * *

Fin de Siècle

Life went on, but with no more sentimental 'romances'. Despite the Court's elaborate rituals and displays, magnificent in appearance but obviously hollow and without significance, Court life dwindled, as an old woman, anxious and often uncertain, wandered her palaces. Her faithful courtier, Sir John Harington, reported in October 1601:

> It is an evil hour for seeing the Queen ... . She is quite disfavoured, and unattired, and these troubles waste her much. She disregardeth every costly cover that cometh to the table, and taketh little but manchet [bread] and succory [chicory] pottage .... She walks much in her Privy Chamber, and stamps with her feet at ill news, and thrusts her rusty sword at times into the arras in great rage.

Her personal vanity was protected by her ladies, who hid the palace mirrors. Ben Jonson reported the gossip that 'Queen Elizabeth never saw herself, after she became old, in a true glass; they painted her, and sometimes would vermilion her nose.' A modern commentator, John Guy, remarks on the 'sense of fin-de-siècle' characterising these last years of her reign.

A German visitor, Paul Hentzner, saw the Queen at Greenwich in 1598, and described the elaborate ritual attending her at chapel and dinner, and remarked on her white, low-cut silk dress, covered with jewels, pearl earrings 'with very rich drops', and a small crown on her red wig. He also remarked on her remaining black teeth. The French ambassador also encountered her:

> She was strangely attired in a dress of silver cloth, white and crimson ... [with] slashed sleeves lined with red taffeta, and was girt about with other little sleeves that hung down to the ground, which she was constantly twisting and untwisting. She kept the front of her dress open, and one could see the whole of her bosom, and passing low, and often she would open the front of her dress with her hands, as if she were too hot ... . On her head she wore a garland of rubies and pearls, and beneath it a great reddish-coloured wig, with a great number of pearls ... . Her bosom is rather wrinkled, but lower down her flesh is exceedingly white and delicate as far as one could see ... . As one could see all her belly, and even to her navel ... . As for her face, it is ... long and thin, and her teeth are very yellow and irregular ... . Many of them are missing, so that you cannot understand her easily when she speaks.

Another foreign visitor observed that 'her bosom was uncovered, as all the English ladies have it till they marry.'[19] The Maiden Queen, still maiden, betrothed only to England.

On 27 December 1602, Harington, to cheer her, read her some amusing verses he had written, 'whereat she smiled once, and was pleased to say, "When thou dost feel creeping time at thy gate, these fooleries will please thee less; I am past my relish for such matters."'

Her last days were spent at Richmond Palace, where she took sick. A former maid of honour reported:

> afterwards in the melancholy of her sickness, she desired to see a true looking-glass, which in twenty years before she had not seen, but only such a one which of purpose was made to deceive her sight; which glass being brought

her, she fell presently exclaiming at all those which had so commended her, and took it so offensively, that all those which before had flattered her durst not come in her sight.

When Cecil anxiously told her she must go to bed, she smiled contemptuously and told him, 'Little man, little man, if your father had lived, ye durst not have said so much: but thou knowest I must die, and that maketh thee so presumptuous.' She resisted death to the very end, and refused to nominate her successor (though the council announced that she had chosen King James of Scotland); and died on 24 March 1603.

Soon after her death, Cecil wrote to Harington that Elizabeth had at times been 'more than a man, and, in troth, sometimes less than a woman'. His words almost echo the criticisms currently directed at fashionably cross-dressing women, such as Mary Frith. The creaking gender system, under pressure exacerbated by the monarch being a woman, strained socio-sexual roles and perceptions, from the lowest to the highest. As for Elizabeth, normal love, sex and marriage were not for her; a normal woman was something she was never able to be.

Notes

Chapter 1: Hearts on Fire

1. Fulke Greville poem: *Penguin Book of Renaissance Verse* (*PBRV*), Woudhuysen, H. R., ed., (Harmondsworth; Penguin, 1992), p. 210
2. Sir John Davies poem: Ibid, p. 252
3. Drayton: Ibid p. 139
4. Harassment: Capp, Bernard, *When Gossips Meet: Women, Family and Neighbourhood in Early Modern England* (Oxford: Oxford University Press (OUP), 2003), p. 227
5. Sayer: Emmison, F. G., *Elizabethan Life Morals and the Church Courts* (Chelmsford: Essex County Council, 1973), p. 212
6. Somers: Ibid, p. 236
7. Orgasm: Stone, Lawrence, *The Family, Sex and Marriage, 1500-1800* (London: Weidenfeld & Nicolson, 1977), p. 489
8. Barnfield: *PBRV*, p. 304
9. Rowlands: Pritchard, R. E., *Shakespeare's England* (Stroud, Sutton, 1999), p. 228
10. Nashe: *PBRV*, pp. 253-63
11. Fletcher: Haynes, Alan, *Sex in Elizabethan England* (Stroud: Sutton, 1997), p. 70
12. Finch: Hubbard, Eleanor, *City Women, Money, Sex and the Social Order in Early Modern London* (Oxford: OUP, 2012), p. 107

Chapter 2: Men About Town

1. Rowse, A. L., *Simon Forman. Sex and Society in Elizabethan England* (London: Weidenfeld & Nicolson, 1974) and Traister, Barbara H., *The Notorious Astrological Physician of London* (Chicago and London: Chicago University Press, 2001)
2. Whythorne, Thomas, ed., James M. Osborne, *The Autobiography of Thomas Whythorne* (Oxford: OUP, 1962)
3. Carr: Hubbard, pp. 94-5

Chapter 3: How to Get Married

1. Breton, *Cornucopiae*, Cook, Ann J., *Making a Match. Courtship in Shakespeare and his Society* (Princeton: Princeton University Press, 1991), p. 81
2. Discourse: Hubbard, p. 255
3. Gawdy: Cook, Ann, J., p. 45
4. Breton, profit: Ibid, p. 43
5. Manners: Laslett, Peter, *The World We Have Lost* (London: Methuen, 1965), p. 91
6. Guazzo: Cook, Ann, J., p. 25
7. Stockwood sermon: Ibid, p. 73
8. Whetstone: Ibid, p. 74
9. Poor maids: Hubbard, pp. 58-97
10. Nan's ballad: Hammond, Paul, *Figuring Sex between Men, from Shakespeare to Rochester* (Oxford: Clarendon, 2002), pp. 51-2
11. Whitney: Pritchard, R. E., ed., *Poetry by English Women, Elizabethan to Victorian* (Manchester: Carcanet, 1990), pp. 26-30
12. Newbie: Cressy, David, *Literacy and the Social Order* (Cambridge: Cambridge University Press (CUP), 1980), p. 264
13. Go-between: Cook, Ann, J., p. 106
14. Rhodes contract: Gowing, Laura, *Domestic Dangers. Women, Words and Sex in Early Modern London* (Oxford: Clarendon, 1996), p. 160
15. Clear: Emmison, *Morals*, p. 230
16. Nuttall: Adair, Richard, *Courtship, Illegitimacy and Marriage in Early Modern England* (Manchester: Manchester University Press, 1996), p. 143
17. Gray: Emmison, *Morals*, p. 4
18. Breton, widows: Cook, Ann, J., p. 127
19. London widows: Hubbard, p. 238
20. Marry a young man: Ibid, p. 250
21. Gouge: Ibid, p. 250
22. Rowlands: Ibid, p. 251
23. Packer; Emmison, *Morals*, p. 10

Chapter 4: Married Life

1. Marriage homily: Stone, p. 138
2. Woman as deputy: Hubbard, p. 113
3. Gouge: Stone, p. 314
4. Tilney: Goodman, Ruth, *How to be a Tudor* (Harmondsworth: Penguin, 2016), p. 265
5. Sexual inhibition: Stone, p. 314
6. Guazzo; Ibid, p. 83

7. Savin: Schnucker, R. V., 'Elizabethan Birth Control', *Journal of Interdisciplinary History*, 1975, Vol. 4, p. 4
8. Ray, paradisal: Aughterson, Kate, ed., *Renaissance Women: A Sourcebook* (London & New York: Routledge, 1995), p 103
9. Vaughan defence; Gowing, pp. 85-6
10. Morilla; Moulton, I., *Before Pornography. Erotic Writing in Early Modern England* (Oxford: OUP, 2000), p. 216
11. Hunt's wife: Emmison, *Morals*, p. 18
12. Married woman ballad; Burford, E. J., *London, The Synfulle Citie* (London: Robert Hale, 1990), p. 141
13. 'Thou sittest'; Rowlands, *The Knave of Clubs*, quoted by Hubbard, pp. 134-5
14. 'a wife hath won': Ibid, p. 130
15. Defences of women: Pritchard, *Shakespeare's England*, pp. 38-41

Chapter 5: Outside Marriage

1. Transgressions: Stone, p. 524
2. Jane Wright: Emmison, *Morals*, p. 79
3. Hunthatche: Adair, p. 83
4. Lysby: Emmison, *Morals*, p. 83
5. Occupy: Picard, Liza, *Elizabeth's London* (London: Phoenix, 2004), p. 193 and McClure, N., ed., *Letters and Epigrams of Sir John Harington* (Philadelphia: Pennsylvania University Press (PUP), 1930), p. 151
6. Barton: Burford, p. 122
7. Stanwell: Haynes, pp. 11-13
8. Cream: Picard, p. 192
9. Susan More: Hubbard, pp. 80-5

Chapter 7: The Heart and Stomach of a Queen

1. Sexual deviant: Hackett, Helen, *Virgin Mother, Maiden Queen. Elizabeth I and the Cult of the Virgin Mary* (London: Macmillan, 1995), p. 142
2. Incestuous relationships; Shell, Marc, *Elizabeth's Glass* (London & Lincoln: University of Nebraska Press, 1993), *passim*
3. Seclusion: Whitelock, Anna, *Elizabeth's Bedfellows. An Intimate History of the Queen's Court* (London: Bloomsbury, 2013), p. 3
4. Elizabeth poem: Pritchard, *Poetry*, p. 19
5. Haydocke: Pritchard, *Shakespeare's England*, p. 26
6. Song, Sweet Bessie: *PBRV*, p. 92
7. Ambassador and Robsart: Whitelock, p. 35
8. Hawkins: Levin, Carole, *The Heart and Stomach of a King: Elizabeth I and the Politics of Sex and Power* (Philadelphia: PUP, 1994), p. 89

9. Inventory: Hibbert, Christopher, *The Virgin Queen. The Personal History of Elizabeth I* (Harmondsworth: Penguin, 1990), p. 100
10. Elizabeth complaint: Whitelock, p. 90
11. Elizabeth and Philip II's sister: Levin, p. 133
12. Willing to marry: Whitelock, p. 119
13. As some noise her: Levin, pp. 73-80
14. Master Hatton: Whitelock, p. 149
15. Elizabeth poem, Monsieur: Pritchard, *Poetry*, p. 21
16. Tichborne poem: *PBRV*, p. 630
17. Deryck: Emmison *Morals*, p. 42
18. Lopez: Whitelock, p. 279
19. Rye, William B., ed., *England as seen by Foreigners*, (Smith, J. A., 1865)

Select Bibliography

Adair, Richard, *Courtship, Illegitimacy and Marriage in Early Modern England* (Manchester: Manchester University Press, 1996).

Alberti, Leon Battista, *Hecatomphilia, or the Arte of Love* (Italy, 1598).

Aubrey, John, ed.; Oliver Lawson Dick, *Brief Lives* (Harmondsworth: Penguin, 1962).

Aughterson, Kate, ed., *Renaissance Women: A Sourcebook* (London & New York: Routledge, 1995).

Berry, Philippa, *Of Chastity and Power: Elizabethan Literature and the Unmarried Queen* (London: Routledge, 1989).

Betts, Hannah, '"The Image of the Queene so quaynt": The Pornographic Blazon' in Walker, Julia, M., pp. 153-84.

Bray, Alan, *Homosexuality in Renaissance England* (London: Gay Men's Press, 1992).

Burford, E. J., *London, The Synfulle Citie* (London: Robert Hale, 1990).

Camden, Carroll, *The Elizabethan Woman* (London: Cleaver-Hume, 1992).

Capp, Bernard, *When Gossips Meet: Women, Family and Neighbourhood in Early Modern England* (Oxford: Oxford University Press, 2003).

Carey, John, ed., *John Donne* (Oxford: Oxford University Press, 1990).

Clark, S., *Amorous Rites: Elizabethan Erotic Verse* (London: Everyman, 1994).

Cook, Ann Jennalie, *Making a Match: Courtship in Shakespeare and his Society* (Princeton: Princeton University Press, 1991).

Cook, Judith, *Dr Simon Forman: A Most Notorious Physician* (London: Chatto & Windus, 2009).

Cressy, David, *Literacy and the Social Order* (Cambridge: Cambridge University Press, 1980).

Doran, S., *Monarchy and Matrimony: The Courtship of Elizabeth I* (London: Routledge, 1996).

Doran, S., 'Why Did Elizabeth Not Marry?', Walker, pp. 307-59.

Emmison, F. G., *Elizabethan Life: Disorder* (Chelmsford: Essex County Council, 1970).

Emmison, F. G., *Elizabethan Life Morals and the Church Courts* (Chelmsford: Essex County Council, 1973).

Fabricius, Johannes, *Syphilis in Shakespeare's England* (London: Jessica Kingsley, 1994).

Fletcher, Anthony, *Gender, Sex and Subordination in England, 1500-1800* (New Haven and London: Yale University Press, 1995).

Freedman, S., *Poor Penelope: Lady Penelope Rich* (Bourne End: Kensal Press, 1983).

Goodman, Ruth, *How to be a Tudor* (Harmondsworth: Penguin, 2016).

Gowing, Laura, *Domestic Dangers: Women, Words and Sex in Early Modern London* (Oxford: Clarendon, 1996).

Guy, John, *The Reign of Elizabeth I: Court and Culture in the Last Decade* (Cambridge: Cambridge University Press, 1995).

Hackett, Helen, *Virgin Mother, Maiden Queen: Elizabeth I and the Cult of the Virgin Mary* (London: Macmillan, 1995).

Hammer, Paul, 'Sex and the Virgin Queen. Aristocratic Concupiscence at the Court of Elizabeth I', *Sixteenth Century Journal*, Spring 2000, 31.1. pp. 77-97.

Hammond, Paul, *Figuring Sex between Men, from Shakespeare to Rochester* (Oxford: Clarendon, 2002).

Haynes, Alan, *Sex in Elizabethan England* (Stroud: Sutton, 1997).

Hibbert, Christopher, *The Virgin Queen: The Personal History of Elizabeth I* (Harmondsworth: Penguin, 1990).

Howard, Jean E., 'Women as Spectators, Spectacles and Paying Customers', Kastan and Stallybrass, pp. 68-74.

Hubbard, Eleanor, *City Women, Money, Sex and the Social Order in Early Modern London* (Oxford: Oxford University Press, 2012).

Ingram, Martin, *Church Courts, Sex and Marriage in England, 1570-1640* (Cambridge: Cambridge University Press, 1987).

Jardine, Lisa, 'Boy Actors, Female Roles and Elizabethan Eroticism', Kastan and Stallybrass, pp. 56-67.

Kastan, David Scott; Peter Stallybrass, eds., *Staging the Renaissance* (London and New York: Routledge, 1991).

Laslett, Peter, *The World We Have Lost* (London: Methuen, 1965).

Levin, Carole, *The Heart and Stomach of a King: Elizabeth I and the Politics of Sex and Power* (Philadelphia: Pennsylvania University Press, 1994).

Loughlin, Marie H., ed., *Same-Sex Desire in Early Modern England* (Manchester: Manchester University Press, 1988).

McClure, N., ed., *Letters and Epigrams of Sir John Harington* (Philadelphia: Pennsylvania University Press, 1930).

MacFarlane, Alan, *Marriage and Love in England, 1300-1840* (Oxford: Blackwell, 1986).

Moulton, I., *Before Pornography: Erotic Writing in Early Modern England* (Oxford: Oxford University Press, 2000).

Nashe, Thomas, ed., Stanley Wells, *Selected Works* (London, Edward Arnold, 1964).

Newman, Karen, 'City Talk: Women and Commodification: *Epicoene*', Kastan and Stallybrass, pp. 81-195.

Palliser, D. M., *The Age of Elizabeth: England under the late Tudors, 1547-1603* (London: Longman, 1992).

Picard, Liza, *Elizabeth's London* (London: Phoenix, 2004).

Pritchard, R. E., ed., *Poetry by English Women, Elizabethan to Victorian* (Manchester: Carcanet, 1990).

Pritchard, R. E., ed., *Shakespeare's England* (Stroud, Sutton, 1999).

Quaife, G. R., *Wanton Wenches and Wayward Wives: Peasant and Illicit Sex in Early Seventeenth Century England* (London: Croom Helm, 1979).

Rose, Mary Beth, *The Expense of Spirit: Love and Sexuality in English Renaissance Drama* (Ithaca: Cornell University Press, 1988).

Rowse, A. L., *Simon Forman: Sex and Society in Elizabethan England* (London: Weidenfeld & Nicolson, 1974).

Rye, William B., ed., *England as Seen by Foreigners* (Smith, J. A., 1865).

Schnucker, R. V., 'Elizabethan Birth Control', *Journal of Interdisciplinary History*, 1975, Vol. 4.

Shell, Marc, *Elizabeth's Glass* (London & Lincoln: University of Nebraska Press, 1993).

Stone, Lawrence, *The Family, Sex and Marriage, 1500-1800* (London: Weidenfeld & Nicolson, 1977).

Traister, Barbara H., *The Notorious Astrological Physician of London* (Chicago and London: Chicago University Press, 2001).

Turner, James G., *Schooling Sex: Libertine Literature and Erotic Education in Italy France and England, 1534-1685* (Oxford: Oxford University Press, 2005).

Walker, Julia M., ed., *Dissing Elizabeth: Negative Representations of Gloriana* (London: Duke University Press, 1998).

Whitelock, Anna, *Elizabeth's Bedfellows: An Intimate History of the Queen's Court* (London: Bloomsbury, 2013).

Whythorne, Thomas, ed., James M. Osborne, *The Autobiography of Thomas Whythorne* (Oxford: Oxford University Press, 1962).

Wilson, Violet A., *Queen Elizabeth's Maids of Honour* (London: Bodley Head, 1922).

Wilson, Violet A., *Society Women of Shakespeare's Time* (London: Bodley Head, 1924).

Woudhuysen, H. R., ed., *The Penguin Book of Renaissance Verse* (Harmondsworth; Penguin, 1992).

Index